Beware of the Dog!

The Two Sides to the Puppy Dog Tail

Julia Day

Bourne and Willow Publishing

*To all dogs who have patiently trained their
owners to love them even after they chewed
holes in their favourite cashmere jumpers.*

Contents

Prologue

July 26th, 2017

Three alarm bells had rung in quick succession. Each slightly more disturbing than the last.

The third and final death knell took the form of an SOS text message from my daughter:

'OMG. DOG IS MISSING. THINK HE'S RUN AWAY. HELP.'

There was no way I could offer any practical assistance. The dog had chosen his moment to abscond to ensure maximum dramatic impact, as seconds before the ping of that gut-wrenching text, the island fort where my husband and I were celebrating our twentieth wedding anniversary, had posted the morning's second distress signal:

'Due to the severity of the sea state, all guests will to be trapped indefinitely until an evacuation craft can safely reach us.'

Under different circumstances, this might have been a golden opportunity – stranded together in the midst of a dramatic storm, in an isolated, romantic hotel, but this trip was proving to be a long way from that starry-eyed idyll. Instead, with a rising sense of panic, I was racing to the nearest gangplank, ripping off all my clothes and preparing to dive headlong into the churning waters to risk the swim to shore. An impulse made even more compelling by the first alarm bell of the morning.

Over what should have been an indulgent breakfast of sky-stacked patisseries, washed down with multiple mugs of freshly brewed coffee, I was having to swallow the suggestion by my husband that we might like to:

'Discuss the sea-state of our marriage'.

It was quite clear that he was referring to a stomach-turning maelstrom rather than a gently rippling mill pond.

The combination could not have been more toxic. Powerless to offer practical assistance in the search for our missing dog and sensing that the full brunt of the incoming storm might smash what remained of our marriage on the rocks, I was desperate to escape our luxury fortress. It is safe to say that this wasn't quite the anniversary treat I had been hoping for.

But, more importantly, WHERE THE HELL WAS

THE BL**DY DOG?

*

Spoiler Alert

Five years post-puppy – June 2020

The evening was perilously perfect. Gently stroked by the warmth of a Midsummer breeze, my black Labrador sat faithfully at my feet as we gazed contentedly across a landscape of ripening fields and clear blue skies.

NOW LET'S STOP RIGHT THERE.

Tempting as it is to prolong that glossy snapshot of 'woman and Dog' harmony and pretend that it perfectly defines the past few years of dog ownership, that would be a kennel load of far-flung balls from the truth.

Instead, I'm going to drag you with me through the deep and prickly hedges of puppydom, with only the slightest of apologies to any idyllic dog-owning fantasies that might get scratched along the way, until maybe, just *maybe*, we come out with a grazed but stoic grin on the other side.

Five years into the roller-coaster ride of dog

ownership, I'm still being pulled in all directions, clumsily dodging an endless volley of curved balls. There have been many days when I've been desperate to press the emergency stop.

For just a moment though, on that idyllic summer's evening, in the company of a dog who was fleetingly capable of behaviour that to the casual observer might pass as civilised, I was feeling dangerously smug.

Inevitably, such blissful reverie was to be cut dead within an instant.

One moment, the dog was genteelly sniffing the warm summer breeze; the next, he was obsessively burying his nose in the nearest bush. With a look of unadulterated glee, he raced to gulp down a desiccated and utterly putrid bacon sandwich before I stood a chance of snatching it from his slobbery chops.

It was probably weeks old.

Almost certainly going to make him sick later.

Undoubtedly, it would be me that was going to be clearing it up.

And this was the easiest that life with my much-loved dog had ever been.

JULIA DAY

*

Just before the poop hit the fan

Five Years Earlier – Autumn 2015

The only sign that something might be afoot on the dog owning front was the mysterious appearance of a dog bowl on my kitchen floor.

As far as I was aware, we did not own a dog at this point, or even a thirsty cat. We had not openly discussed the possibility of such an addition, and, despite prolonged interrogation, no one in the household would confess to the purchase.

The truth of the matter is that the dog bowl was just the final straw in a long campaign by my husband and kids to drag me kicking and screaming into dog ownership after years of subjection to an impressive array of persuasive techniques, designed to slowly scratch away at my '**NO DOGS**' resolve. At the time of writing, I am *almost* converted - but let's not get ahead of ourselves - this has been one hell of a journey and the trials should not be underestimated.

So, let's get a few things straight:

Firstly, I am not a dog person. Or at least, not a *real* dog person.

Compared to those impressive born and bred dog-worldly types, with well-trained working dogs trotting at their heels, I am closer to a badly trained con artist. Five years in and I am still experiencing a serious case of impostor syndrome.

Pre-dog, my pet owning experience as a fully grown adult was limited to an undeniably ordinary menagerie, that has included:

- A random collection of goldfish
- My children's hamsters
- My husband's tropical fish collection
- Three feisty and free-spirited rescue cats who ruled the neighbourhood with claws of steel.

Not one of these offered anything like an adequate training ground for what was to hit us when the dog arrived on the scene.

Most importantly, these pets of the past did not require training. Shaking a tub of goldfish flakes and watching your highly precocious goldfish rise to the surface doesn't count. Nor does adopting a rescue cat and teaching it to come to the shake of a box of cat crunchies. All three of our cats trained us to serve them as soon as they realised that we would attend to their every desire and were therefore deemed worthy of hanging out with. They were far too superior beings to be controlled by mere mortals and would probably have eaten us alive if they were any bigger and slightly peckish.*

*Disclaimer – no pet of ours has ever expired at the hands of another pet, and no family member has ever been consumed by a giant cat.

Still, best not to take any chances.

And so it was, that no matter how hard I tried to cling to those carefree days of goldfish ownership and feline subjugation, a faithful, trusting and eminently trainable dog was to enter our midst. (The latter part of that sentence *may* turn out to contain something akin to a dubious truth and a pack of lies, but I'll let you be the judge of that.)

With such questionable dog-owning credentials and a deep-rooted reluctance to take on this challenge, you may well wonder why on earth such a non-dog person would let herself be dragged into this. And that really is the whole point of this tale. The call of the puppy has the power to override all logical thoughts and all their infinite variations and I *genuinely* believed that I was immune. There was no way on earth that a dog was going to make its way into our family.

In fact, I knew I was immune because I had evidence to prove it:

The **NO DOGS** resolve had held fast through twenty years of marriage and fifteen years of parenthood. It was not cracked by almost everyone we knew succumbing to accessorising themselves with sensible non-allergenic labradoodles. ('Sensible' really translates as very cute and on-trend but we are far too polite to say that out loud.) Nor was it softened by an infinite tide of dog-owning propaganda in the form of endearing puppy pictures, shared with me over social media by my children, which, rather than melting my heart, brought on waves of nausea linked to visions of destructive chewing and uncontrolled bowels. The thought of getting up on a dark, wet, winter's morning to march a dog around a muddy field and pick up its poo overrode all fantasies of wholesome family walks. Even a week's holiday in Wales with my children's newly adopted, completely imaginary, and therefore perfectly trained dog (it waited invisibly and remarkably patiently with them outside shops and reliably retrieved sticks on the beach) did not pluck at my heartstrings. It did however get us some weird looks, but how were any of us to know that in a not-so-distant future, hanging around outside shops with only one member of your family allowed to enter at a time was to become one of our most highly rated experiences?

Anyhow, crystal ball gazing aside, the bottom line was that I REALLY didn't want the responsibility of a dog. As much as I love them and had grown up with a run of fabulous and faithful Labradors, I was just starting to glimpse a freer future ahead of me. The kids were growing up and after years devoted to motherhood, the opportunity to work more flexibly and step into a life that wasn't entirely focussed on childcare and housework was almost within my grasp. With my husband having worked unpredictable shifts for years, jobs or even taking an evening class had been logistically challenging with no family nearby to help. Maybe time as a couple was once again on the horizon? Perhaps weekends away without the complications of babysitting and planning. Spontaneity! Freedom! I could almost taste it...

Surely this was not the time to get ourselves another responsibility and tie for what could be a decade or two? PLEASE, NO!

But the universe didn't appear to be listening.

Out of the blue life threw us an unexpectedly large and bouncy curved ball.

Attached to the ball was a spirited and energetic black Labrador puppy.

There was no turning back.

January 1st, 2016

For me, the inevitable journey to becoming a dog-mother started the night of a neighbour's New Year's Eve party.

Of course, it would be completely reasonable to assume that the indulgences and celebrations of such a night might lead to a weakening of any long-held resolve, but in this case, at least to start with, it was only made more solid.

My schoolgirl error was in my choice of attire – specifically, choosing to wear a pair of jet-black velvet trousers to the party. Our hosts had recently succumbed to the temptation of a pure white Alsatian puppy - a clash that the more style conscious might have easily foreseen, but regrettably, this wasn't on my radar. This puppy, despite her cute and glamourous exterior, suffered from a serious case of FOMO and as such, insisted on partaking fully in all the celebrations. Despite maintaining an impressive sobriety, as the night wore on, she socialised endlessly, even flirtatiously rubbing herself against my trousers and accessorising them with layers of long blonde highlights, masterfully outstripping anything I'm ever likely to achieve through my hairdresser. Under different circumstances, I might have taken this as a compliment, but the tenacity with which her gift remained attached proved nothing more than a timely reminder that I REALLY DID NOT WANT A DOG.

Under no circumstances would I be falling for the fluff factor and cute website photos that had shattered my friend's timeworn defences.

Except that's not quite how things turned out.

The following morning, whilst tending to my trousers with reels of sticky tape, delusional with the fantasy of maintaining my resolve, I remained blissfully unaware that at that exact moment, in a home not that far away, a little black Labrador puppy was just hours from entering the world. He may not have been destined to change the colour of my trousers but within weeks he would irrevocably change our lives.

How this could be about to happen?

Put simply, life twisted in such a way that suddenly, not only did we have a family majority wanting a dog, but we ended up realising that we genuinely needed one. Fate had finally decided to laugh in my face and counter every defence - rest assured, the universe is nothing if not creative in the infinite forms this joke might take.

In our case, my husband Doug found himself having to leave his job and the tie of shifts at all hours of the day and night due to a long-term and increasingly problematic back condition. With infinite long days alone stretching ahead and desperately hoping to rebuild some degree of fitness after a series of operations, a dog seemed to be the answer. Or at least, it did to him.

Fruitlessly, I tried to suggest that the conversational ability of a dog would not necessarily provide the level of interaction that he desired, or that it may cramp his style should he wish to go out for the day. Even that the dog might jerk randomly and cause him more discomfort. But this all fell on deaf ears. Doug wanted to try to walk further than the end of the road and felt that the obligation and sense of normality of doing this with a dog would be the only reasonable way to force him out. It would be a distraction come pain or shine – sorry, terrible pun, but there is an element of truth behind it. He assured me that the dog would attend training from an early age and so there would be absolutely no issue with pulling, barking or any other undesirable doggy habit. Flashbacks to the hours of training my parents had put in with our childhood dogs made it hard to fully share this confidence, but reluctantly, I could see he had a point and secretly acknowledged that the alternative of leaving him alone moping in the house with no impetus to leave and hours with just himself for company was an even more worrying scenario. We had two teenagers who were equally enthusiastic about dog ownership, and I was working part-time so surely everyone would pull their weight on this?

There was just one problem: I had been the family gatekeeper to dog ownership for so long that the lock was rusted. To say no and maintain my resolve would have risked resentment, and quite possibly been detrimental to Doug's health, both physically and mentally. But to oil the lock and open the gates might let in the hounds of hell…

Damn it.

What should I do?

Cornered, and with my back firmly against the

wall, I had no choice but to tentatively turn the key.

Not fully of course, and **very, very** slowly as they painfully creaked to sound of my muttered profanities at what a fool I must be.

Bizarrely, the pack of yapping puppies that I had imagined would rush through the narrow opening and land delightedly in our laps didn't immediately appear.

I stuck my head through...peered out into the darkness and looked around.

Still nothing.

Perhaps I just needed to squeeze through the gates and take a closer look. Maybe venture just a little bit further out; after all, I could always turn back...

At this point what is really needed is a large STOP sign.

Or perhaps just some traffic lights to give a little

pause for thought…

But I didn't have either of these, or even some crucial but easily ignored small print:

DO NOT ever kid yourself that you can simply step back from the viewing process.

Should I say that again? A little louder perhaps?

DO NOT ever kid yourself that you can simply step…

No, sorry, that would be rude and completely futile, because who really who wants to read the small print?

But don't say that I didn't warn you.

For those of you who are more detail orientated here's some well-intended small print for you to skim over based on a real-life case study of a close friend:

- **Never pick a puppy when bereft with grief over the sudden loss of your much-loved pooch. Especially if in your desperation to fill the gap, you find your replacement pooch via a quick internet search and then proceed to ignore the fact that the 'breeder' has a rotting sofa in the front garden, the pup was removed from its** mother at 3 weeks; the pup is now four months old and the best description the seller can offer in terms of its socialisation is the fact that the dog saw another dog on the beach once. Oh, and when you turn up to meet it, the dog barks extremely viciously at you – it really would be best not to overlook those clues.

Unless the following appeals:

Adopting a puppy that is so terrified of everything that you will have to give up your job to train and care for it, finance endless sessions with dog psychologists and for a while you will be obliged to wear luminous jackets around the house to alleviate pups fear of workmen. Just saying.

Or how about this one:

· An American friend of mine found himself in a car with his ex-wife and three teenage children, embarking on a 2000-mile round trip to collect their new puppy. Yup – that was 2000 miles. Surely extreme even by American standards? And this was not even going to be *his* new puppy – all puppy stroking pleasure would be reserved for the children and his ex-wife. His role was simply chauffeur-cum-support driver, and it was very clear that he was there on sufferance, the first choice of co-driver being infected with a dangerous and highly contagious virus…who'd have seen that one coming? Whenever driving duties were not required, he was to be pushed to the rear row of seats and out of everyone's way. You may think that travelling across the USA with your ex-wife and kids to pick up a puppy is something that could never happen to you. It's madness, right? Could destroy already delicate relationships. Well, think again. Such is the power of the call of the puppy.

Otherwise, stick with the large print.

*

They seek him here; they seek him there...That damned elusive Labrador!

Having admitted, even if only to yourself, that dog ownership is a distinct possibility, it is important to take control of the situation.

Think about the important questions: What breed of dog to consider? Rescue dog or pedigree puppy? Who are you and what would suit your lifestyle?

If you bypass this part of the process, it is quite possible that the first puppy you view, whether it be the a trendy pug (my son's preference as they seem to be the essential accessory to any future YouTube star, or a Dalmatian (my daughter's as apparently it could be trained to run alongside a bike – a terrifying proposition in my mind but there you go), it will be your companion for the next ten to fifteen years. The speed at which you can move from casually viewing a puppy to taking it home can be as little as five minutes if my market research is correct.

You will tell yourself that passing a winter's evening googling dog breeders and researching breed characteristics is just harmless fun.

IT IS NOT HARMLESS and like many things that are fun, it has its dark side.

The cute puppy photos will invade your mind and adjust your psyche. Before you know it, the surfing will become an email, maybe a phone call. If you're lucky, perhaps this 'perfect puppy' will no longer be available, and so, let off the hook, the search can continue commitment-free.

For now.

Because unless you have the credentials of an undercover Secret Service Agent and the foresight to lock yourself away, ensuring your search history is thoroughly deleted (incognito mode would have been well worth a thought here but sometimes the thrill of dancing on cliff edges proves too much to resist), it is very likely that such activity will have been spotted by other family members.

In my case those aforementioned rusty gates creaked so loudly that I was caught out almost immediately. Inevitably, it will be the most dog adoring member of the family who will expose your behaviour and, such will be the level of delight at their discovery, that no level of bribery in exchange for their silence will be sufficient. If you really are the last line of defence against a canine invasion, this should be avoided at all costs. In this I failed abysmally.

Still, having been caught out, my best advice, other than rapidly developing an allergy to dog hair, is to embrace the situation and focus on the finding the right puppy.

This we thought, was going to be a walk in the park. We would google a couple of local breeders from the array on the internet, pop along for a visit and ask all the right questions. We would then instinctively pick the right puppy and all live happily ever after.

Not so much a walk in the park as a wild goose chase with a distinct lack of goose. *

* By the way, for those of you who are already irritated by my compulsion to scatter predictable dog related clichés into this, TOUGH. I'm having a great time and will pack them in at every opportunity. 'Pack' was not one in case you were wondering.

Anyway, back to the ~~tail~~ tale in hand.

Sometimes a friendly phone call to a couple

of breeders produced nothing but a dismissive and non-committal grunt in response to the recommended question list that we'd so carefully curated. Some took a couple of weeks to respond and when they did, the response failed to answer any of our questions, setting off alarm bells that couldn't be silenced. The thing is, how do you tell the decent breeders from those irresponsible puppy farmers out to grab your cash and palm you off with a pup, torn too early from its mother, who in turn is possibly forced to endure a life as a breeding machine?

Identifying the perfect puppy was proving quite difficult.

Not only did we need to find an available and suitably raised litter, but it turns out that if you are lucky enough to find a genuine breeder, you then need to go on a major charm offensive to prove that you are going to be able to offer the pup the lifestyle that it deserves. Not only did we have to tick all our boxes, but we also had to tick all of theirs.

Tick boxes for us:

- Intelligent enough to be trainable. Not so intelligent that it suffers from boredom after a millisecond and turns to destruction of all the home-furnishings the minute our back is turned.

- Friendly personality. Although not over friendly. Dogs humping the legs of visitors is awkward for all concerned, except perhaps the dog.
- A 'man's' dog that Doug wouldn't feel embarrassed to be seen out with. By this we mean it must be a reasonable size. This will also mean that we are less likely to trip over it. Though not so big that it takes up half the house or so strong that it will pull us into hedges.
- No piercing barks. In fact, no fierce and threatening deep barks either. Unless we're being burgled. So, a quiet canine capable of differentiating between friends and foe would be just the thing.
- The right image - Not gimmicky or too trendy. Don't want anything that looks like a fashion accessory but needs to fit with who we are. Who are we?
- Able to walk decent distances but not hyperactive.

Somehow, after deeply considering all these criteria, inputting them into dog matching algorithms, researching breed characteristics and watching the full range of dog-related programmes on the television, it turned out that what we wanted was…

A Labrador!

Well, there's a surprise.

It turns out that choosing a dog is a bit like choosing a pair of shoes. You go out open to all the options, try a diverse range of possibilities, whilst genuinely believing that you will come back with something a little different this time. What really happens is that you come back with the first pair you tried on which are pretty much exactly the same as the last pair you bought.

Having grown up with Labradors the die was cast. Of course, there was still the matter of colour and gender to choose – perhaps we could deviate from black boys and go for a golden girl?

Just in case you were wondering, we didn't. Black Labrador. Male. Exactly what I grew up with.

Surely you can't go wrong with a Labrador?

*

To rescue or not to rescue, that is the question?

Morally, offering a good home to a dog in need seems like the right thing to do. What's more, we were told in no uncertain terms by my husband's aunt, during the wake of a family funeral, that this is the *only* option that we should consider, and due to the sensitivity of the occasion, it did not seem appropriate to contradict her or admit to leaning towards a less morally palatable option. The number of homeless dogs out there with heart-rending background stories is huge and being in the position to offer a loving home and a lot of time to one of these dogs made it a serious consideration. The aunt in question had set the bar very high in this regard, managing a household that currently incorporates rescue dogs and cats saved from streets stretching across Europe from Swansea to Geneva. This didn't seem like the moment to discuss our preference for a straightforward pedigree puppy with a perfect hip score.

We had looked at rescue dogs. We had. Honestly.

In fact, I'd even rung up one charity to enquire about visiting a promising sounding 18-month-old Labrador who was being fostered locally. During a very helpful conversation with charity's coordinator, we were told how this dog had been rescued as a half-starved and abandoned puppy from the streets of Romania and was now a strong-willed young male who needed a dominant owner to look up to. I put down the phone and began to wonder if we were biting off more than we could chew. She had explained that this dog's dominant tendencies would need to be worked on with experienced owners. We were prepared to try, but at the end of the day, we were in many respects first-timers. The Labradors I'd had as a child were always my dad's responsibility. Doug has never had a dog and his mother's long line of rescued Alsatians had on occasion provided such a terrifying welcome party that we were almost too scared to get out of the car. Obviously, this would never have been used as an excuse to justify turning on our heels and heading home as soon as we'd arrived. That would *never* have crossed my mind.

Nonetheless, I began to dread the call back offering us an appointment to view this dog as this would take us to another level of commitment that I wasn't sure we were ready for, yet to dismiss the dog without even a visit seemed like we weren't giving him a fair chance.

It wasn't long before the call came through, with the apologetic explanation that 'Victor' had had to be removed from the foster family as the carer was very ill with morning sickness. He was now in kennels in Norfolk and although we were welcome to drive up to meet him, it seemed as though fate had taken this decision out of our hands. I breathed a huge sigh of relief.

Back to the internet. By this stage we had found that most of our enquiries just led to dead ends. How could it be this difficult to find a healthy, well-cared for puppy with a well-intentioned breeder?

It turns out that we'd probably been looking in the wrong places and it was only by chance and some random late-night surfing, that rather than heading off to pick a dog from a back street puppy farm, we found ourselves on the doorstep of a newly approved Kennel Club breeder with a litter of Labrador puppies that had become available to view only minutes before I miraculously stumbled across them. With perfect hip-scores and a five-generation pedigree we had discovered the closest thing we could get to a dead cert.

At this point I was still completely oblivious to the speed at which puppies like this find decent homes and so whilst the breeder must have thought I was incredibly informed and serious, in reality, I had simply blundered my way towards our perfect dog. Finally, we had struck puppy gold!

With the pick of the litter at our fingertips, going to view and pick a puppy was now a race against time. Decisions were racing through our minds – was it reasonable to pull a sickie from work the next morning to go and pick a puppy? Could I trust this life impacting choice to Doug alone? How will we know which is the right dog for us?

The days of turning back were over. Within 24 hours Doug and my sister (whose dog credentials far surpass my own and I was too much of a wimpy swot to take the sickie*) had picked out a chubby little black boy with friendly eyes and the air of a lazy gourmand. I believe it took them under four minutes to pick out the pup, pay the deposit and send me a photo.

Unashamedly thrilled, I couldn't help but show the little fellow to the nearest person in the staff room – a student teacher who became so excited about our new addition that she immediately exclaims with unbridled delight that "This must be one of the most exciting days in my life" and "If I ever need a dog-sitter, please just ask!"

I make a strong mental note of this.

And that was how easy it was for our fates to be sealed.

* I know, I know. I really need to awaken my inner rebel, but it's hard to teach an old dog new tricks!

*

The Days of the Dog

Saturday 30th January – The first family visit

Our first family visit to greet our future puppy!

The thought of meeting the adorable little ball of fluff who was going to become our best friend for the next few years filled us with a rosy happy-go-lucky euphoria. Any thoughts of the potential challenges that a new puppy might present had been pushed firmly out of mind. Today was far too exciting to dwell on such minor details.

How we had reached this point of no return in four short weeks, still eludes me, but by this point I can honestly admit to being genuinely excited. Nervous excitement perhaps but thrilling nonetheless; and as we drove what felt like an interminable hour to meet him, we really had no idea what to expect.

The breeder doesn't disappoint. Her home, despite providing care and shelter for three children, a husband, two adult dogs and six puppies, is immaculate - the sort of immaculate that I couldn't imagine achieving even if I lived alone with a full team of staff, and the puppies couldn't look happier. The mother is gentle and happy to meet us and although our pup is only three weeks old, he is already the biggest of the litter and speeding ahead of his siblings in the race to grow. I shamelessly indulge in a ridiculously proud potential dog-mother moment, admiring his genius in the guzzling stakes before we spend a few minutes, utterly enthralled, as he scampers about the pen to explore the garage floor with his litter mates.

He has an endearing fascination for shoelaces.

He also demonstrates an exceptionally scientific interest in brooms.

And blankets.

In fact, anything within paw-padding distance.

Chewing these things seems to make him incredibly happy. We guess he must be ready for his next meal and that this is a passing phase that will no longer apply by the time we get to take him home.

We gaze and stroke him adoringly.... only 5 weeks to go until he is all ours!

Saturday February 6th

A week later and we can't resist going back for more. We have convinced ourselves that this is an essential trip to deliver a toy and a blanket that smells of us in the hope that this will ease the transition away from his siblings and mum when the time comes, but really, we just want to see him and give him another cuddle. Four weeks to go and he has already more than doubled in size from when we first picked him out. What a boy!

What's more, we have named him – no longer will he be known by his pedigree name of Kylo, the fiery dark warrior from Star Wars.

Should we have read more into this...? No, that would have been silly.

From here on in, meet 'Radar'.

For those of us with long enough memories, this was not intended to be a reference to the character from M.A.S.H., nor was it anything to do with the dog in Fireman Sam. It was simply an appropriate echo of Doug's former life as an Air Traffic Controller, where he spent many years keeping dots on a radar screen at safe distances from one another. In his new life, Radar would turn out to be an even more complex challenge but at this point we are just relieved to have agreed on a name.

I could stop there and pretend that this perfect choice of name just leapt into our laps and everyone simultaneously agreed whilst sharing a self-congratulatory group hug and stroking each other's egos. But it wasn't quite like that.

With four future dog parents in the family, there were automatically twice the number of opinions than when we were picking out names for the children, and even then, we learned very quickly that releasing such information before the definitive reveal opened us up to a barrage of conflicting 'helpful opinions.' As it was, we had to consult a very long list of dog names downloaded off the internet and cross check the short list against the following standard commandments:

- Do not pick a name that sounds like a command.
- The name should be no more than two syllables long to prevent the dog from becoming confused. Not to mention the embarrassment of shouting something long-winded like 'Lord Muttkins of Slobbery Chops' across the countryside every time the dog chases a rabbit.
- Ideally the name should start with a high-pitched sharp consonant sound

like 'Sh' or 'Ch', and end in a long 'ee' sound. So, you could always shorten the above to 'Slobbery' or 'Choppy'. Or not.

· Think carefully before naming your dog after a family member. Or at least secretly indulge yourself with the thought of this before opting for the name of a celebrity dog perhaps?

Simple!

Friday 4th March: D(og)-Day

I freely admit that despite all my previous reservations, I can't wait to bring our new puppy home today. This feels a bit like the day we brought our babies home from hospital except that this time I haven't had to go through hours of labour. And this is a dog, so surely, with no multiple night-time feeds or endless nappy changing, this will be an easy ride compared to the terror of suddenly finding yourself responsible for a helpless human being?

Within minutes of arriving to pick him up it is becoming clear that I might have underestimated some aspects of how easy this is going to be.

Before even leaving the house, Doug and I found ourselves falling into the same protective and obsessively prepared pattern we had with the children: Travel crate disinfected and secured, blanket neatly folded, towels for accidents at the ready. Except that this time, before we can take our new arrival home, we must remove the young fellow from his mother and siblings and hope that we can provide a worthy equivalent. This shouldn't be heart-rending but trust me, it really is. Perhaps it was because we were first-timers or maybe it was a natural response to having seen him play so happily with the other puppies just moments earlier, but we couldn't help but feel that our tentative attempts to provide a comfy blanket and a cuddly toy were paltry consolation. The exchange was friendly and straightforward, but this was perhaps tricky for the breeder too. It was, after all, their first litter and no doubt letting the pups go after all the energy and care they had put in, was as much of a difficult moment as a relief.

Radar sits on my lap all the way home, dismissing the expensive and carefully chosen chew-resistant plastic bone, preferring to chew on a little bit of scrap rubber that he had scavenged from the garden as we scooped him up. While I try to keep him calm and safe as we drive the hour home, Doug drives as if I'm carrying a priceless Ming vase on my lap. I desperately hope we can live up to the challenge we've taken on. Radar sits unperturbed, enjoying watching the world go by and occasionally proffering a friendly lick. It seems though, if nothing else, we have a dog that enjoys travelling. This bodes well as we have already booked a family dog-orientated holiday in Devon this August, which will entail a drive of at least four hours. Along the A303. Including the Stonehenge bit. So, he's going to really need to love cars.

The first night

We have a perfectly fool proof plan for this. We have read every book with a section on settling your new puppy into your home and have all bases covered. All bases that is, except getting any sleep ourselves.

So much for my thoughts on that.

We decide that we should sleep next to his crate on the sofa-bed, which being by the back door, means we can pop him outside for a wee last thing at night and then once again a few hours later if he wakes up. Radar thoughtfully sticks to this plan impeccably and particularly enjoys his early hours excursion to the garden. In the hours between, we lie still, not wanting to disturb him; anxiously listening to him shuffling and breathing, in the hope that he is not too cold or lonely away from his doggy family.

I'm pretty sure that this was not how I envisaged life with a dog and wonder fleetingly if perhaps we are a little overprotective. I vow that tomorrow night we will try to be more practical and let him sleep without us by his side. Neither the thought of signing ourselves up to a Hobson's choice of 15 years of sleeping on a sofa bed by the back door attending to his every need or having him join us in our bedroom upstairs are options that I am ready to embrace at this point and so standing our ground seems to be the way to go.

The first day

By mid-morning, our son Charlie declares that life with a new puppy is not quite how he imagined it either. Admittedly, he had been particularly fond of the gentle affections of our ageing cat whose quiet purring and self-sufficient nature didn't impinge on his gaming or destroy his shoes. A needy puppy with a compulsion to chew anything precious or dangerous was a responsibility level that he was not quite ready for.

By lunchtime, after four hours of non-stop family

fun retrieving chewable treasures from Radar's jaws, Charlie was sufficiently traumatized to declare that this was *definitely* the *worst* family decision that we had ever made.

Clearly the situation needed addressing. I was trying hard to hide it, but my nerves were beginning to fray slightly too. I, at least, had been slightly prepared for what lay ahead and knew, having had dogs before and raised two children, that time would see us through, but there is nothing easy about having a young and lively new addition in the family.

We opted for immediate extraction to the nearest dog-store for a little retail therapy and to choose a toy to entertain the new arrival with that would distract Radar from his fondness for our more treasured possessions.

As it turned out, the nearest dog store also happened to be a high-end Orvis outlet with a tempting array of some of the most luxurious dog products on the market. We were spoilt for choice as I winced at the cost of the antler chews and stylish country-style tuggers. My human children had got through their early childhood with hand-me-down toys and boot sale bargains. But the dog was clearly in a different league and was going to be spoilt rotten.

The second night

The puppy-loving student teacher has helpfully suggested that we place a ticking clock near our new-arrival at night to help him feel that his mother is close. She clearly is a dog-whispering genius as, along with a carefully wrapped hot water bottle, this works a treat. Or at least, it works a treat until a couple of hours after midnight, when we begin to hear some whimpering. The whimpering doesn't stop and our stealthy attempts to check he's ok without being spotted fail immediately. Leaving him to cry is almost unbearable and in the end my daughter and I can quell our maternal instincts no longer. We both leap out of bed at the same moment, decide enough is enough and begin to head downstairs. At this very moment, perhaps sensing that he has proved his point, pup stops crying and goes off into a deep sleep until the almost civilised hour of 6 am.

At this point we remain blissfully in denial of the level of control that our new arrival is already having over us.

Day three

The blissful ignorance didn't last long.

Today, Doug and I dared to leave the house for 30 minutes to get some shopping, leaving pup with Sascha, our eldest and generally exceptionally reliable daughter.

We return to find that pup has taken over the armchair in the lounge and is issuing brave barky noises from his new throne, while Sascha cowers on the edge of tears and terror on the other side of the room.

This is not how we pictured life with our puppy.

Week 1

This is just like having a new baby. I am not exaggerating. The memory of those early days as a young mother is firmly etched on my mind and I am having shocking flashbacks. This time round though, I am raising a species that is not my own and sadly there is no allowance for maternity leave for dogs. This wouldn't have even crossed my mind as being an issue, after all, Doug is at home full-time and young puppies seem to sleep as much as they play, but trust me, IT IS A BIG ISSUE.

A puppy may not be just for Christmas, but there could be a definite advantage to welcoming one into your home at the beginning of a prolonged holiday period. I would recommend at least a month, although a six-month sabbatical or enforced confinement to home, should such an opportunity ever present itself, might work nicely.

Instead, I am faced with a different reality.

There are still four weeks to go until the next school holidays, when my fantasy of two weeks of freedom, along with the presence of a couple of teenage off-spring to help spread the load, will become a reality.

Ok, no it won't. Because it is a fantasy. I know this in a deep and not-prepared-to-accept kind of way, but let's not go there for now. Hope is important.

In the meantime, the puppy dictates a strict routine of two hours of play, alternated with two hours of rest. Let me make it very clear though, that the rest is for him, not us. In fact, the play is also for him, but he thoughtfully invites our involvement. If this sounds reasonable, then I really must bore you with a little more detail.

The two hours on are *FULL* on.

If I turn my back, or even if I don't turn my back, pup will chew my favourite shoe. This happens even if have spent the previous two hours of 'rest' hiding all the shoes.

It is not just the shoes.

The rug in the lounge is rapidly becoming a favourite chew toy and even though we have rolled it up and stuffed it under the sofa, he takes endless pleasure in testing the scratching and tearing capacity of his claws on the rough underside. If it is pushed further out of reach, he does not hold this against us but simply experiments with the durability of the underside of the sofa. The wooden legs of a much-loved family sideboard are also a firm favourite. We have this in common, but for different reasons.

It also turns out that despite our attempts to clear the house of anything precious or dangerous that might not be suitable for Radar's jaws, we have failed big time. He proves this by cleverly bringing us a new treasure to admire every few minutes. On the upside, he is probably the one member of the household who actually notices and attempts to remedy my many lapses in domestic perfection. In this respect, he will fit in perfectly and in my sleep-addled state and exhaustion from maintaining such high levels of vigilance, I am in a small way, feeling a warm sense of camaraderie with him over this.

It rapidly fades…

This level of vigilance to keep our puppy, home and possessions safe is tricky at the best of times, but by a typical yet unexpected twist, it coincided with me being not only busy at work, but also totally overrun at home with three ghost-writing projects that I was helping with, all suddenly needing to be completed at the same time. This ideally requires many peaceful and uninterrupted hours in front of the computer. All I can say about this is that if I got three minutes, I was lucky. The rest of the family are trying to distract him, but it is amazing how creatively he manages to escape their attention to discover a new location for his fun.

Tiring Radar out is proving nigh on impossible and there are still three more long weeks until he gets his second set of injections, which will allow him to go out for walks beyond the garden.

Week Two

The garden.

To preserve what remains of our somewhat shredded sanity, the garden has become our sanctuary. Fortunately, we have been blessed with dry weather. The alternative is not worth considering and should only reasonably be considered by those who have survived something along the lines of a Duke of Edinburgh Gold award expedition in torrential rain, a camping holiday in the UK in 'summer' or extreme survival training.

To be clear about this, the situation is not as bad as some might imagine i.e., that the dog has taken over/destroyed/reassigned the interior of our home to the exclusion of his adoring owners. That would be just silly. No, our displacement in daylight hours is purely a way to allow him to let off steam. He has a lot of this and visions of Icelandic geysers, that, if it wasn't for the cost of said dog, I could afford to visit, are both an appropriate metaphor for that steam and a suitably distracting image if a shift of focus is required.

Anyway, enough of thoughts of escape to an Icelandic spa and scenery beyond that of our backyard. The preparation of the back garden alone has depleted all the energy and funds that such a trip would require.

Our first job was to secure the garden. On careful

inspection of the boundaries, we identified four possible escape routes. The first was a narrow 15 cm gap between two fence posts under a hedge. This may not seem that wide, but I'm not prepared to take any chances. I have already been trained in counter-escape techniques by my human children as they proved that trying to follow a pint-sized explorer through a hole in the hedge as a fully grown adult, in a school playground surrounded by super-mums whose offspring don't move so unpredictably, doesn't end well. Or at least it didn't end so well for me - the only upside of the dragged-through-a-hedge-look was the extent to which it prepared me for what was to come with the dog. The kids were having a great time. Less said about this the better.

And so, with a resigned sense of déjà vu, I crawl under the surprisingly wide hedge whilst narrowly avoiding losing an eye on a spiked branch of pyracantha. I block the gap with a firmly positioned log.

The next two gaps lead behind the garage and with some creative recycling involving a recently dismantled side-gate, a small fence panel and some chicken wire, we also manage to puppy-proof that particular escape route.

Probably.

Can puppies jump?

Surely not.

This only leaves one remaining gap, and it is the widest of all.

Five metres to be exact.

Five metres of open access to the rest of the world that is no longer even cut off by the side gate *or* the worryingly low fence panels *or* the five-bar gate across the driveway. These were clearly nowhere near secure enough to prevent the escape of our precious new Houdini and so have been temporarily replaced by some flimsy plastic fencing held up by a metal pole loosely poked at a jaunty angle into the grass until the installation of our new, solid, 5ft high garden gates.

I am unexpectedly excited about the new gates as they should not only protect us from losing the dog, but they will transform the back garden and give us a refreshing degree of privacy. They are not perhaps quite as exciting adventures I could have afforded with the - stressed cough - unmentionable price tag associated with this installation, for which I am still in shock. Four figures are at least one too many to swallow comfortably. Let's speak no more of this. I'll just have to wait a bit for those adventures. After all, it's not as if international travel is going to banned any time soon is it?

OK, so obviously, theses escape fantasies couldn't begin to compare with the joys of a secure and private garden and Radar thoughtfully proves this by not only showing how fun his newly enclosed garden is to explore, but by doing this under the cover of darkness. This is such a great game with a jet-black silent-pawed puppy in a garden that I can highly recommend it. What made it particularly thrilling was that whilst the garden may well be secure, it is packed full of overgrown bushes and a surprisingly deep pond.

Can puppies swim…?

We loved the thrill of not knowing where he would pop out from next or even if, in his wild and untrained state, he would even know to respond to our desperate calls for a sighting.

Resorting to a trick that may well work for hungry lions and had previously been tested successfully on the cat, a quick shake of the food bowl brought him out from his cover. We subsequently invested in a flashing red light collar attachment, which is most becoming and proves how inspired we were with his choice of name.

The next 3 weeks

Somehow, we make it through our period of confinement. Never has a trip to the vet for his second and therefore liberating set of injections been so highly anticipated.

Any fears on whether he might take umbrage at having a needle stuck into him and go on to develop a lifetime fear of veterinary surgeons were barely surfacing. This was the gateway to freedom and we were rattling it in desperation.

Turns out, Radar quite liked the vet. And if I'm honest, I'd become rather fond of him myself. Not only did he possess a beautiful Irish accent that reassured me as much as the dogs, but as a farm vet in rural Hampshire, every visit felt like a step back in time. This was not a high-tech corporate style surgery - just a traditional family run practice with a farmyard for a car park and a waiting room that had been warmly and seamlessly run by the same receptionist since I first came with our now long passed cat, over 10 years ago.

When I say warmly, I mean the friendly welcome more than the ambient temperature. Even on a bitterly cold winter's morning, the receptionist remains resolute in flipflops with nothing more than a small fan heater to counter the draughty surrounds, but then she is clearly made of hardier Hampshire stuff than me, as a mere Essex import.

Now, finally, we can take him out on proper dog walks. Ones that will tire him out and give us some down time. Gone will be the days of him weeing all over the lawn turning it into a spotty mess of burned brown circles, and randomly deposited piles of sticky poo will no longer make crossing the lawn feel like navigating a mine field. The future is bright and sunny and packed full of congenial family walks!

Well, that was *our* plan.

Radar, it seemed had a slightly different one.

For a start, he reminded us very clearly that until he was a little older, he really shouldn't be expected to walk too far as this may damage his hips and cause him problems in later life. He was of course quite correct on this point but what he thought of as 'too far' was anything further than fifty metres from his food bowl. This dedication that he exhibited to his health and well-being seemed a little extreme and his reluctance to negotiate hinted at a disquieting level of stubbornness. Probably just a puppy thing. He'd grow out of it. Surely?

For now though, the journey to open fields, which would normally be a mere two minutes' walk from our front door, was taking a little longer.

The first challenge was the stretch from the front door to the pavement - a gap of maybe 15 metres. At this point it seemed that the concept of a destination was something that had figured little in Radar's mindset. To him this was all about the journey, and that 15 metres offered endless opportunities for exploration.

Firstly, there was the threshold between the house and the wider world. Here, according to the law of the dog, one should stop and pause, sniff the air momentarily and then twist around on your lead a little; perhaps to check that there is nothing new happening inside before taking the next step.

It is then far better to take a random course (I was tempted to say zig zag but even that would have been too structured) through the garden. There were tree stumps to sniff and car tyres. Neighbours coming out to offer strokes and adoration, maybe a stretch of gravel to roll in...

It reminded me momentarily of my parents' philosophy with us as young children, that it was important to explore the country on your doorstep before rushing off to far-flung exotic destinations. I consider embracing this concept but figure that I'd been doing so for so long that we were at risk of being institutionalised. What's more, my parents were so much more liberal than our Labrador, exposing us to a whole nation of excursions rather than Radar's strict Stay-At-Home policy. Little did I realise that our dog was showing a respect for his health and an instinctive need to train us for an as yet unknown future where such behaviour would see us through much darker days.

But that was not yet for us to know.

We just wanted to get to the field.

Instead, I stood outside my neighbour's house while Radar rolled on his back on the sun-warmed cobbles, giving himself the doggy equivalent of a hot stone massage. If I wasn't already feeling slightly humiliated, I would have been tempted to join him...always fancied booking in for one of those. Generously though, Radar didn't insist on the massage taking a full hour, and after 5 minutes or so of rolling and rubbing he felt so relaxed that he allowed us to turn tail and walk the few metres home. No rush. The field could wait...

Do they specialise in hot stone massages at Icelandic spas?

24 hours later (Sunday 24th April)

I have a plan. This will undoubtedly outwit the puppy and extend our 15 metre parameters of freedom.

Instead of turning left and risk passing (ha! If only!) the hot cobblestones, we will turn right. I have carried out a mental risk assessment of this expedition and I'm confident that the route is clear of such temptations. In addition, a full hour or two has been set aside so that we can proceed at his pace. My aim is to get to the other side of the village and possibly climb a hill where I'm pretty sure a conveniently placed dog poo bin and bench can be found at the top.

We begin our expedition at 11.09am.

The journey to the pavement goes remarkably smoothly and by 11.13am we have reached the pavement. Even turning right instead of left doesn't cause Radar any undue concern. In fact, very soon, he begins to quite take to this excursion. Or at least he seems willing to proceed. It appears that the reason for this is that if you are a small puppy exploring a village on a Sunday morning for the first time, the world smiles at you, acknowledging you for the hero you were born to be. No sooner had we met one adoring fan, then there was another to sniff just around the corner.

Such adoration does mean that Radar was far too thrilled and excited with discovering his high rank in society to lower himself to publicly relieving himself, but he did at least proceed at a random pace through the village and before long, we had even crossed a road and reached the bottom of the hill. For a few moments, we continued at a moderate trot, until his impeccable behaviour and soft brown eyes lock with those of a lady trimming her bush. She politely stops her work to drop to her knees in front of Radar and proceeds to tell me that they are thinking of getting a dog. Possibly a rescue dog... and how was it having a new puppy?

This was a tough call.

Fleetingly, I considered telling it as it is (sleepless nights, exorbitant security costs to keep your captor safe as he imprisons you in your own home whilst also wreaking havoc on it), but this seemed a little extreme. Should I embellish the positives and tell her how delightful it is to have a sweet young puppy in your life? I take a deep breath and proffer a middle ground, advising 'give the matter very careful thought because delightful as he is, a dog really can take over your life', adding that training a puppy is tough at the best of times so I wasn't sure how easy it would be with a rescue dog. Perhaps the look on my face was enough without words, but I never did see them with a puppy and so I fear I may have put them off…

We headed home, not quite making it to the bin and the bench, but I take comfort in the idea that even the great conquerors of Everest must repeatedly head back down and acclimatise before making the final ascent. We travelled almost half a mile and return home by midday before resolving to make another attempt on the summit tomorrow.

For the remainder of the afternoon, I promise myself a therapeutic Sunday treat of taming the garden.

Gardening

I'm pretty sure that any dictionary worth its sort would agree that gardening can reasonably be defined as:

Gardening (Verb): An activity involving the creating, cultivating and caring for an attractive outdoor space.

It would definitely *not* be anything along the lines

of:

Gardening (verb): Chasing the broom and grabbing the bristles viciously between your teeth every time it moves, pouncing on rakes, digging holes in the grass, emptying the contents of the green waste bag in search of a good stick to chew, sticking your nose in the grass and smelling it with such intensity that you create a lawn decorated with miniature muddy bunkers or biting through juicy looking stems especially those daring enough to be holding up an carefully cultivated flower head.

I almost want to repeat that alternative definition multiple times, because the reality of my afternoon was that I had to endlessly experience this 'endearing' (yes, my teeth are gritted) behaviour.

This was not the therapeutic experience I had been intending. Perseverance might have its place but quitting to head inside for coffee and cake seemed to be more than reasonable. Until I was joined by Sascha who sits alongside me and says affectionately, 'Mum, you smell of Radar!' The smile on her face and warm tone does little to avoid the fact that I have just been told that I smell of dog. Is this better or worse than those almost long-forgotten days of smelling of regurgitated baby sick? I'm not sure.

Monday 25th April

As the saying goes, 'It takes a whole village to raise a dog', or something like that. And so it is, that as I am zigzagging randomly (yes, an *actual* zigzag this time!) in Radar's unpredictable wake on our next attempt to conquer the hill, I realise that by a remarkable stroke of good fortune, I am surrounded by some of the country's greatest minds in dog rearing. What's more, they are all terribly keen to support my path from helpless newbie to proficient professional. What luck!

Today, as Radar alternated between leaping gleefully and casually rolling around on the ground to get himself twisted in his lead, we were fortunate enough to cross paths with la crème de la crème of local dog society. A pair of professional, working cocker spaniels whose credentials extended way beyond the local fields to the distant and hallowed halls of Crufts no less. The contrast of their obedience to the wild exuberance of my puppy was stark. It was hard to imagine that even an entire village would be enough to raise us sufficiently in the ranks of dignified doggy behaviour to reach such dizzy heights. Still, it was early days and perhaps based on the rather obvious distinctions of his breed and energy, they recommended that I sign Radar up for gundog training. Thoughts of the challenges faced as he joined puppy training classes in the gentle environs of the village hall flash across my mind.

He wasn't exactly the perfect student...

It turns out that taking your dog to puppy training classes is just as hard as taking a toddler to playgroup. Admittedly, you don't have to battle with the puppy to put his shoes on – thank goodness - can you imagine?! No, it simply requires a whole new level of competitive parenting combined with significant shaming potential. Unlike toddler groups where you might be rewarded for your efforts in attending with a consolatory cup of tea, biscuits and a weekly dose of speaking to other adults whilst the children play under a collective watchful eye, puppy training has no such luxuries. Your puppy may well be more enthusiastic than many toddlers at this rare chance to socialise, and in the case of Radar, lacked any shyness that his human siblings might have felt. He was desperate to join in and say hello, invent new games and pretend not to hear any of the instructions. None of which was allowed.

The only treat that was allowed, was in fact, treats. And that was just the problem.

This dog was capable of being so good for a treat that it was like having a child who would tidy their room, do their homework and help with the washing up before you'd even got out bed. As long as you fed them nothing but Pick & Mix. Translate the ensuing doggy equivalent of a sugar high into whatever picture of highly energized puppy you like, and you'll get pretty close to the challenges faced.

What's more, the attention span of a puppy is short at the best of times and Radar appeared to have better things to do with time than subject himself to the will of this dictatorship. He might *just* have made it through a class of thirty minutes maintaining some degree of respectability, but a whole hour was way beyond what he was prepared to accept - it was a weekly trial to keep him focussed and under control during those last long minutes.

With this thought hovering nervously at the front of my mind, I struggled with the suggestion of the gundog classes. Visions of this being the SAS version of puppy training, including the guns flashed before me as I smiled and nodded, whilst secretly vowing to focus on the more achievable goal of one day graduating from the puppy beginners class to improvers. Even this felt like a moon-shot, but then so was Everest.

Wednesday 27th April

Today was the first outing using our latest dog accessory – the extendable lead. I'm not sure if the impetus for this purchase was to give us or the dog a greater sense of freedom. Perhaps in our naivety, we imagined it would be a win-win for all parties.

That's not quite how it panned out.

Certainly, Radar benefitted from being able to extend his range beyond my arms stretch, and perhaps I should have been grateful for the improved early warning system that it gave me of his tendency to rapidly jerk in unexpected directions. However, what I gained in foresight was lost threefold in control. Perhaps I was getting something wrong, but at this point in time I am in desperate need of advice on how to avoid the following issues:

- How not to become entangled in metres of extended lead.

- How to avoid the dog becoming entangled in the lead.
- How to avoid the lead getting dragged in the mud as soon as the dog changes pace. And no, it DOES NOT retract perfectly before getting caked in everything he wanders through.
- How to avoid having your hands cut to shreds when trying to pull him back in an emergency (these leads with their flat razor-edged retractable tape do not lend themselves to passing smoothly through tightened fists).

May Day Bank Holiday weekend

Something about this week that was uncannily idyllic. The sort of week that makes you glad to have a dog and realise how blessed you really are.

It all started on Monday, which was not only the May Day Bank Holiday - a good start to any week - but the weather was turning drier and in full holiday spirit, we were going on a super adventure with the dog!

This was to be our initiation into the realm of the traditional English Country Show where there was billed to be falconry, gundog trials, jousting, dog agility demonstrations and live music as well as side stalls selling all sorts of delicious doggy treats and accessories. Well, delicious if you're a dog I guess – boar chews aren't really my thing. Giddily, we imagined how happy this would make Radar and what excellent socialisation and stimulation this could be for expanding his horizons. From the second the car doors opened, his enthusiasm was palpable. In every direction there was another Labrador or Spaniel; all trotting around like they owned the place. What am I saying? They did own the place. Without them the event would have been entirely pointless and for Radar, no other attraction was needed other than the opportunity to smell the backside of every dog he could lay his nose on. He cared little for the overly competitive ones showing off in the trials, or the hoops that the more agile could jump through. He showed a passing interest in an unusual demonstration of how to catch a rabbit with a rather large and worn net, but probably felt he could have done a better job without it, given the chance. The treats however were politely received and grudgingly accepted as a small bribe to entice him to kindly abstain, on occasion, from pulling the lead with such enthusiasm that I was at risk of a dislocated shoulder. But with every passer-by unable to resist admiring his endearing expectation to be adored, who can blame him?

Don't get me wrong, it really was a fun afternoon out, though fun in much the same exhilarating but exhausting way as a day at a theme park with the kids. Fortunately, with a dog you can enjoy the warm parental glow of indulging your fur-baby*, without him begging for 'just one more ride' just as your energy reserves hit zero. Radar just wagged on happily and settled down for a short kip in the car for the journey home.

*Fur baby – I had never heard this expression before a friend of mine claimed she had lost hers in a Facebook post. Feeling some level of concern for whatever predicament had befallen her I discovered that a fur baby is actually a much doted-on pet - in this case her new puppy. Hmm. Not sure I'll be using this phrase again in a hurry.

Tuesday May 3rd

There is something magical about a warm early summer's evening that can relax your guard in a way that little else can; and so it was, that by the end of this week, I was ready to take a step into the brave new world of letting him off the lead for the first time outside the garden. With back up in the form of a friend with a delightfully well-behaved dog, or at least one that was perfectly primed to come back to the call of a tasty treat, we let him free. Miraculously, Radar didn't bolt at the first chance for freedom but stayed close and almost seemed to enjoy our company. I know in my heart of hearts that what really happened was that the treats stuffing our pockets - handmade by my friend from liver fresh from the butchers - were utterly irresistible to my greedy pup and there was no way he'd stray far from such delicacies. But another part of me will pretend it was down to great training and our ever-growing bond. Nothing wrong with a little healthy disillusionment.

Wednesday May 4th

Things just get better and better. Such is the improved level of maturity from Radar that this-evening I was able to take him to his first piano lesson.

Well, ok, as much as it might be interesting to be raising the first canine piano protégé...oh, hang on a moment...this might not be as rare as you think – wasn't there a dog in the muppets who was particularly talented in this regard? Yes! Rowlf – it's all coming back. What a genius and without question my all-time favourite muppet! More of a chocolate brown labradoodley type dog rather than a pure black Labrador though, if I remember rightly. So, Perhaps Radar hasn't quite got the genetic heritage to pull this off?

Anyway, I digress.

Believe it or not, the piano lesson wasn't actually for him; he hasn't quite got the paw stretch. But, as luck would have it, by micromanaging Charlie's lesson to coincide with Radar's walk requirements, we were able to head around the corner to a beautiful stretch of the River Test – the perfect spot for a bit of early evening paddling followed by a rest, legs dangling from the footbridge (my legs, not his – that would have been mean), watching swans glide by in the distance. The happenstance to be adored by two hikers armed with sandwiches kept Radar focussed and momentarily perfectly behaved. I'm pretty sure this is what having a dog is all about.

I remember as a child being told, after one of our dogs was no longer with us, that we would remember the happy times so much more than the difficult ones. I'm feeling quite enthusiastic about this mindset as the day ended with some collateral damage that I'm going to blank out with thoughts of stately swans and a crystal-clear chalk stream.

For the sake of an honest account though I

summarise the loss as follows:

- Total destruction of today's (unread) copy of The Guardian
- One pot of sour cream: Stolen, attacked and sprayed around the lounge
- One newly purchased climbing plant shredded across the main stem
- One baguette stealthily acquired and nibbled before control was relinquished

Saturday May 7th

I guess it had to happen. Maybe the wind changed or perhaps last week was the calm before the storm, but today was a Bad Dog Day.

This is not a world away from a Bad Hair Day. Though it is in fact slightly worse and it is as unlikely to be remedied by a stiff Hair of the Dog as by a decent pair of straighteners.

Waking up with a bad back didn't start things off well. There is nothing worse than knowing that you have no choice but to spend the day keeping a puppy out of trouble and well-exercised whilst being unable to move without shooting pains down your leg. Added to that, today I was solely in charge of dog-sitting duties as my daughter and husband had gone out for the morning and my son was experimenting with being a hormonal and slightly moody teenager who would prefer to avoid parents, siblings and fresh air at all costs. Opportunistically, Radar adopted the mindset of a curious scientist, taking the opportunity of this perfect storm to test the limits of what might be possible under such conditions. He produced an insightful set of results:

1. It is entirely possible that if you approach a lamp post at the right angle and speed you can ensure that your owner is forced to wrap themselves around it in the pose of a tree-hugger, whereby you will win yourself the freedom to pee and sniff for as long as it takes them to extricate themselves. If this is carried out in the most open and central place within the community that you can find, it is very likely that their rush to disentangle themselves from this slightly embarrassing state of affairs will slow down their escape leaving you additional sniffing time.

2. Pooing outside the boundaries of your own garden really can be done. In fact, if you are a dog, it is generally considered

JULIA DAY

quite an accomplishment. However, choosing to place your first public poo in the centre of someone's gravel driveway is not quite right. Especially when that poo is actually two enormous poos, deposited directly outside a kitchen window and when your owner's pockets contain only one small see-through plastic bag. The shame of having your poo paraded through the streets on your return home is beyond bearable, but it is unlikely that your owner will want to draw attention to herself by doing anything more than sharply hissing 'no' for fear of further embarrassment.

3. Even if taken for a walk in the dark, you will not be able to entirely protect your owner from some level of embarrassment. This is particularly true if you insist on prolonged sniffing of bushes positioned outside living room windows just after the sun has gone down. At this point, blinds will not yet be drawn and your owner with feel an intense sense of discomfort, as if they are a stalker, or at best a decidedly nosy neighbour trying not to appear

voyeuristic. The effect of this will be increased threefold if you are a dark-coloured dog – a black Labrador perhaps – as you will remain well hidden behind the aforementioned bush, unlike your accompanying human. Unless they crouch down next to you. But that would just be weird.

Today's collateral damage:

- One plate smashed as pup tried to reach the crumbs on it.
- One T towel and a jumper pulled from the washing line then dragged around the garden.

The evening brought little respite.

I don't think Doug had read the memo on the dog depositing the contents of his bowels on a neighbour's driveway this week. I'm absolutely sure I mentioned this event in passing, as it was undoubtedly a milestone in terms of achieving a significant purpose of the walk, despite being somewhat humiliating. Tonight though, I was hoping to put thoughts of dog poo out of my mind as we were about to head out for dinner with friends and Doug had kindly offered to take the dog out so I could get ready. I gently reminded him of the risks of not taking poo bags with him following the amazing leap in pup's development, but he felt entirely confident that he would not fall prey to the same trauma as me. Raging inside at this illogical approach, I know I should just let him learn the hard way when presented with a giant poo and nothing but a see-through sandwich bag to pick it up in; perhaps he'll be lucky and find a forgotten crisp packet in a coat pocket, but why take the chance? Needless to say, the dog does not subject him to the same level of trauma as I had to endure. In fact, he does a quick wee and pops back in to settle down for the night. I however am still raging and plotting to stuff his pockets with pink scented poo bags when he's not looking. The pink ones are definitely the worst. Smell like toilet cleaner and can be spotted in your hands a mile off.

Ok, enough. It's important at these early stages of dog ownership to remain calm and not let such teething issues come between you and your beloved.

Amazon will deliver the poo bags tomorrow.

Sunday May 8th

In the name of scientific advancement to support future generations of canine companions, I have agreed to participate in a Labrador research programme. It seems that all this should require is the input of Radar's vital statistics at regular intervals. The programme researchers have even sent me a simple video on how to measure a dog's height. This involves watching two vets attaching a sheet of paper to the wall, the dog then stands next to it and as soon as you've marked his height on the paper the dog is free to go, and you can measure and input the height. What could be simpler?

Well, quite a lot of things actually.

The clue should have been in the fact that there were two vets present for the demonstration video and no doubt a hand-picked and suitably obliging dog. I, of course, had neither luxury but by the time I'd realised this, I'd already signed up and Radar was beginning to sense a requirement for obliging behaviour which immediately put me at a distinct disadvantage.

Problem 1: My dog did not want to stand by the wall with paper stuck on it. He does however seem happy to lie at the base of said wall, with his legs in the air. Though not with them sufficiently in the air to allow me to measure him upside-down. In fact, each leg is arranged at a slightly different and ever-changing height, which does not sit comfortably with my need to provide scientifically accurate data. The thought of my inputted results landing Radar with the label of 'scientific anomaly' is too much to bear. I do finally get what I feel is a reasonably accurate measurement, but Doug, who has been observing the process from a safe distance, suggests that it may be around 2 cm out. I am tempted to do something I might regret with the ruler at this point but maintain composure and attempt to measure him with a meter stick from the ground up. The dog that is, not the husband – he would require an additional metre rule and then I'd be so well armed that...

Anyway - back to the task in hand - Radar thinks this is inspired and is greatly entertained by the game of preventing me from making such a measurement by grabbing my 'stick' and attempting to chew it.

Repeatedly.

Problem 2: The research also requires that we submit a weight for the dog each month. I am rapidly losing interest in scientific research by this point as I consider the options: Persuading Radar to balance all four paws on a set of bathroom scales OR lifting what will very soon equate to a fully grown 25Kg dog in my arms and subtracting my weight from the total, whilst ensuring I can read the scales accurately from a standing position with a large dog in my arms obstructing my view.

I'm slightly ashamed to say that my resolve to support Labrador science wavered and irretrievable collapsed after inputting the first set of rather questionable results.

Tuesday May 10th

I have had an epiphany.

It is time to indulge in some self-help, doggy style.

Now, don't get the wrong idea here. This is all about expanding my mind in an educational and nurturing manner.

I have decided to embrace the ever-growing canon of dog-related literature to help me to see beyond the challenges of early puppydom and improve my understanding of the canine mind. What better place to start than inside the mind of the very lovely Ben Fogle whose demeanour alone is enough to warm the cockles at the heart of any storm.

His book 'Labrador' is a delightful account, taking in the history of our nation's beloved Labradors whilst carrying the reader on a journey through his own experiences as an owner. It was a book that felt like a warm fire on a winter's night or the kind words a wise friend might utter when you're wondering if things will feel less challenging in the future. By the end of the book, I was not only convinced that I had the best dog in the world but was also proud and grateful for the unexpected chance to be the owner of such a fantastic example of his breed. I can even begin to imagine that everything is going to be just fine...

Encouraged by this, I have started my next read - 'Inside of a Dog' by Alexandra Horowitz - a fascinating insight into the internal workings of a dog's mind which seems like the perfect solution to trying to truly understand what's going on behind those melty brown eyes. But it's going to require to real focus - Horowitz, with a Ph.D. in Cognitive science, is an expert in this field and to get the most out of this I'm going to need an attention span of more than two minutes. So far, I haven't managed to get to the end of a dog day with any attention span left at all. Perhaps this will be one to savour for later.

Weekend of May 14th -15th

A few years back, Doug and I escaped for the first time since having children. It was our 10th wedding anniversary and we had booked an indulgent and romantic trip to Venice, leaving our 5-year-old and 3-year-old with my parents. I hadn't felt so excited about a few hours away for years and couldn't believe my luck; but even now, I recall how nervous I felt leaving them – would they miss us? How would my parents remember the multitude of information I had felt compelled to impart to ensure my children's well-being for two nights? What sort of state would they be in on our return? As it turned out, I needn't have worried; the kids were fine. The parents however were a slightly different matter. Our three-year-old son had been going through a U2 phase. I had been secretly quite proud of his somewhat precocious appreciation of iconic rock but had failed to mention the obsessive nature of his passion to my parents. For most of his waking hours, my dad had been subjected to repeated videos of U2 live at Slane Castle, accompanied by a three-year-old reproducing his version of the vocals. By the time we returned, both parents looked white with stress and left for home within moments of us walking through the front door. Seven years later and we were about to do the same again, except this time we were leaving Radar.

Still haunted by those looks on my parents faces half a decade ago, I didn't dare ask friends or family to dog sit. No, this time we would do the responsible thing and employ one of the most reliable dog-sitters around who had also reliably cared for our rather needy cat every time we went away for years. We planned to be away for just one night to celebrate my mother-in-law's 70th birthday in Wales. We were sure it would be fine. After all, the dog can't sing and had, so far, shown next to no interest in U2.

Twenty-four hours later we returned from the birthday celebrations and instantly recognised the disconcertingly familiar look on the dog-sitter's face: A barely disguised mix of exhaustion blended awkwardly with obvious relief to see us and a well-feigned smile. My heart sank. Had Radar found his inner rock star after all and howled endlessly for hours?

Apparently not.

Radar had however enjoyed a fabulously exciting weekend. So thrilled was he by the opportunity to explore a new home and make new friends, that he had chosen not to waste any of his waking hours sleeping. Instead, he had indulged in the sort of gardening assistance that I had hoped he might have grown out of: Thoughtfully pulling up newly planted shrubs and running around with them playfully in his mouth, pulling on the lead in a desperate attempt to play with other dogs on every walk and then teasing his carers by repeatedly hiding under their sofa to avoid capture. Unsure whether he'd be welcome again, I tentatively broached the possibility of another sleep-over during the August bank holiday, but it turned out they were already fully booked. Funny that.

It seems that yet again, Radar was doing his best to train us for a strict Stay-At-Home policy. Like the kids at school who endlessly enquire as to when on earth they will ever need to use Pythagoras in their future, I looked into Radar's eyes and pleadingly questioned why we needed such training. He remained silent. Clearly implying that I didn't yet need an answer to this question – my job was just to trust that I needed to follow his lead on this. Hmm…time would tell.

Monday 16th May

Generously, Radar seemed to have exhausted his reign of terror the moment we got home, thoughtfully allowing us a few short hours of recovery time from our travels. He even showed glimpses of restraint such as a tail wagging sniff rather than a full-on lead entanglement of dogs and their respective owners as we bumped into old friends whilst strolling around the village. This is one of the many pleasures of having a dog – the chance to say hello and chat with people that you'd never otherwise see; perhaps I'm beginning to see the light. Perhaps Radar was just exhausted after his fun weekend.

Wednesday 18th May

OMG! – Sometimes I wish I had a collection of copies of this book in my handbag to give out to those in need.

Today at work I heard the angst-ridden and resigned confession of one of the feistiest and most determined of my colleagues admitting that it was looking as though family pressure was going to force her into having to finally get a dog. She has been listening to my dog tales for several weeks now, usually with an expression of abject horror on her face. She had previously even stated that she would 'rather die' than have a dog to look after, blatantly aware that such an addition would only add to the pile of daily tasks that fell to her. This is a reality that many dog-mothers must accept, and, in her case, as the lone female in a household of boys, no amount of equality pretence was going to blur her vision on this. In fact, so aware of the potential for imbalance in the everyday split of household tasks, that she even confessed to secretly keeping a small suitcase ready-packed in case she needs to evacuate and abandon her post at a moment's notice. So, how could a woman with such determination and foresight, fall at this final hurdle? The truth is that for most of us, when the crew cajole for long enough, the compromise to keep them happy to avoid a dog mutiny is the conclusion that even the most seasoned skipper will fall prey to. Just saying.

Oh, and don't assume the whole crew have to be in on this – in this case her husband was very much on her side, but the needs of their son were pulling on their heart strings as strongly as a sailor hauls his capstan.

Gosh - I'm suddenly overcome with the urge to sing a sea-shanty – where did that hail from?

Ahoy my friends now please be shore

That y're up to more than a muddy paw

'Cause sea dogs stay aboard for life

And sometimes cause a bit of strife!

Heave-ho and pull that lead…

Ok. Enough. Not sure what came over me there, but you know, I reckon sea shanties really could become a thing…

Clearly though, this was no time for a musical interlude and before I sailed too far off course, it suffices to say that I tried extremely hard to point out that dogs are challenging even with a full-time house-husband and me working part-time, but I don't think that any of my brutal honesty sank in.

Part of me is intrigued to see how this pans out. Will they succumb?

I'll eat my captains peaked hat if they don't.

Friday 20th May

There's nothing like getting an early start in the garden on a bright late spring morning. It is 6.45 am and Radar is using his initiative and ever-improving gardening skills to divide an ornamental grass for me. He has cleverly extricated it from its home, adeptly bypassing the two wooden pallets that I had used to protect the plant from such attacks. I cannot begin to express how helpful it is to have a gardening companion who is prepared to test the robustness of my endeavours so selflessly and to force us to strive for even more rigorous levels of protection. Doug suggests encasing the grass in chicken wire, which seems like an excellent plan and so much more attractive than the wooden pallets that blocked and completely defeated the point of having an attractive grass in the first place. I'm fairly sure this must also have been Radar's point and so I spend a happy hour cutting the wire to size and positioning it carefully around the grass in the most aesthetically pleasing manner.

Radar shows some polite interest in this process

but also remains dedicated to his mission of ensuring that that the plant's PPE is adequate for purpose. What is this about? Why is my dog so concerned about keeping our standards quite so high in the PPE department? Does he know something we don't?

Sorry, I'm clearly overthinking this.

Radar puts the wire mesh concept to the test, and I witness, with a conflicting mix of pride and irritation, its rapid removal with a nimble pawing and accomplished shake of the jaws. He then proceeds to further divide the grass, perfectly emulating the concept more commonly used in biology - the R number that measures the transmission rate of a disease in relation to protective measures used to control it. This dog really needs to chill out. I try to explain that he should be focussing on learning to walk on the lead and playing fetch, rather than trying to plan for a global pandemic or national gardening obsession, but he stares at me as if I'm stupid until I firmly attach the chicken wire, but this time with dog-proof metal clips.

Now he's ready to play ball.

Saturday 21st May

Today, we are off on an adventure which has an uncannily Blytonesque theme to it. Could it be that George's perfect dog Timmy in The

Famous Five may have unwittingly influenced a whole generation of adults into craving canine companionship? Am I needlessly questioning those subconscious biases in writing this book and potentially crushing the dreams of a generation, or should I venture on try to redress the balance with a more realistic view? Hell, who knows? Who cares? Today we are stepping right back into the golden age of steam to witness the return of the Flying Scotsman!

Apparently, it will be passing though the countryside just a few miles down the road from us. After a little research on the Ordnance Survey map, we have worked out that we could park in a nearby village and walk adjacent to the railway line ready to set up camp and see it run past, all whilst timing the whole expedition to perfectly coincide with Radar's need for a walk. Genius!

The plan gets off to a flying start (can you believe I managed to throw that phrase in – Flying Scotsman/Flying Start!? Ha! Sorry. I know I shouldn't laugh at my own jokes, let alone mediocre puns, but I'm not sure that anyone else is going to).

We successfully park up, seemingly away from any mass gatherings of fellow train spotters. Just for the record, train spotting isn't normally my thing, but you know, I haven't got out much lately and it is the Flying Scotsman, so this is totally justifiable.

We manage to wind our way through the cottages to a path that crosses the exact field that we had located on the map and manage to make it halfway across before Radar stops to relieve himself. This of course is exactly what he should be doing, but unfortunately, he chooses this moment to produce the squidgiest and most enormously proportioned pile of poo imaginable. It is one of those poos that is going to fill at least one bag and yet at the same time prove particularly difficult to pick up.

Now, there are many moments as a dog owner that you might find yourself weighing up the rural nature of your location against the difficulty rating of bagging your dog's poo. There have in fact, been those who have publicly advocated the concept of finding a stick and flicking the poo into a nearby hedge, thereby avoiding the polluting effects of the plastic poo bag or the abandoned bulging sacks seen hanging from branches across the nation, however, none of these options were available to me at this time. Firstly, as we were in the middle of the field, there was a distinct lack of sticks and hedges within flicking distance, or even trees to hang bags on. Secondly, despite the rural nature of our location, I was becoming acutely aware that we were not in the least bit alone. As Radar was busy emptying his bowels, I could see that there were increasing numbers of people armed with cameras sporting telephoto lenses surrounding the field. Now, I'm not suggesting for a moment that they had all come out to operate as undercover dog paparazzi, ready to paste our predicament on the front page of next week's issue of the local paper. They may, just possibly, have been training their lenses on the adjacent railway line, but I have to say that the whole situation made me feel an urgent need to unmistakably retrieve the poo. To make my mission even less incognito than it already was, I realised that my pockets were mysteriously devoid of bags and that my daughter was carrying the full family supply, whilst having already successfully distanced herself from us by over 100 metres. If I ran to catch her, I would be seen to abandon and lose the position of the poo and therefore risk the wrath of the Poo Paparazzi and so, with few options remaining, I had to resort to shouting about the incident across the field and incur the wrath of a very put-out teenager forced to retrace her steps to save the day. Of course, there are no poo bins in locations such as these and so on top of all this, we had to carry around a putrid pile of thinly wrapped poop for the rest of the afternoon.

Still, it wasn't long before we had regrouped and were counting our blessings that this whole debacle hadn't occurred once we were settled in the midst of the ever-growing throng of train spotters. Picking a spot from which to watch the flypast, we settled, adding to the throng of lenses. We found a convenient post to which we could attach Radar's lead and placed a towel underneath him to counter the bed of nettles that might have stung his paws. With pockets bulging with treats, and Radar not in the least bothered by the now persistently pouring rain, we gave the impression of having an amazingly well-behaved puppy. He was in his element and delighted to be free to express his inner trainspotting geek.

As it turned out, we got to spot a few more trains than we'd bargained for. As the rain fell increasingly heavily, it became clear that our wait was not to be the 20 minutes we had planned for, but significantly longer. News got through that the Flying Scotsman had been delayed due to people walking on the tracks further north. Rumours as to what this might mean flew through the crowd in a fever of messaging, dodgy phone signals and sudden camaraderie. By the time the Scotsman steamed past, we had been waiting in the rain for nearly 2 hours. In that time, we had seen four Great Western trains pass through and as a special treat…wait for it… two empty local buses went by on the road behind us! Does life get much more thrilling than this? Of course, it wasn't all bad – we successfully managed to fashion ourselves a set of fabulous plastic bag skirts in fetching Sainsbury's orange to wear over our jeans to preserve a little dryness. Not that effective as it turned out, but I can certainly recommend it as a spirit-lifting strategy that will get you some unexpected attention at a train-spotting meet if that's your thing.

Tuesday 24th May

You know when you've been really looking forward to a bowl of cookie dough ice cream….and then it is cruelly snatched from you by a greedy puppy when you turned your back to answer the phone?

I have nothing else to say about today.

Wednesday 25th May

All is forgiven. Radar has seen the light and shown so much improvement in dog training classes that he has now moved up to the improvers class. This is such a proud moment and I think that there is no higher accolade that he or I need to achieve in life. Maybe we can even aspire to quitting classes altogether. Such a lovely thought to go to sleep on…

Friday 26th May

It is 6.30 a.m.

To be fair the days always start at 6.30 a.m. now as Radar, unlike the rest of my household, is very much an early riser. Which is why I have drawn the short straw of joining him for an early morning drip. No, that is not a typo, but the word 'dip' would have suggested something almost pleasant and mutually enjoyable, and this is not quite how the morning was turning out.

Radar, it appears, has suddenly discovered a liking for water mint. Water, I could understand, after all, he is a Labrador; but other than stoically enduring the soaking from last weekend's trainspotting expedition, he has yet to be tempted to dip his paws in even the smallest of paddling pools or gentlest of streams. Even more oddly, his interest in water appears to be predominantly horticultural: Within moments of being let into the garden, he was showing a strange and inexplicable ability to be able to walk on water whilst pulling at clumps of the burgeoning water mint from the garden pond. I watch this miraculous talent for a few seconds, before realising that my dog is not actually walking on water. He is in fact behaving more like a renegade pirate and is daringly walking the plank along the back of the pond to reach his treasured weed before dragging it away to hide under the hedge. No doubt he plans to trade it later for pieces-of-eight-meat. It was therefore somewhat of a surprise to both of us that in the next moment he disappeared with a splash only to re-emerge seconds later having discovered the unknown depths of his doggy paddle and then showering me with this news along with a generous splattering of pond water and duck weed.

Radar chooses this moment to conclude that he is sufficiently refreshed to head inside for breakfast. My attempt to intercept him with a cosy towel receives little appreciation other than the discovery (on his part) of what fun it is to viciously bite the towel that I'm trying to rub him down with. Just for the record, trying to add an additional towel to the mix so that he can keep one between his jaws while I try to dry him with the other one doesn't work. The game is all about the chase.

11.30a.m.

The rest of the family have just about raised themselves from their slumber, but so far, no one has offered to take the increasingly lively puppy out for a walk. I have been his main source of entertainment for the last few hours and to be honest, would quite like someone to give me a break. It seems that the sticking point is a slightly different outlook on the purpose of a walk. For me, I'm keen to save the lawn from piles of poo that could catch you unawares at dusk as well as avoid the small patch of grass that we have, becoming singed and browned with wee. Unfortunately, I'm beginning to realise that I am battling a conflicting philosophy, which aims for the dog to poo before his walk so that the excursion can be enjoyed without having to carry around a bag of excrement. The fact that Radar has so far refused to move his bowels in the garden this-morning, may be the reason that no one else is keen to take him out. I am torn. Should I give in and do it myself before I have a mess to clear up in the garden, or stand my ground and let someone else enjoy a bag-free walk? Of course, as it turns out, it is Radar who forces the issue my making it clear that he has had such a fun morning keeping me busy, that he might soon be in need of a nap. We head for the hills.

6.00 p.m.

Today's toll of scavenged items:

2 walking socks (brand new and unworn)

1 shoe

1 sandal

1 winter scarf (HOW? WHERE FROM? It's nearly June FFS!)

A bag of cotton wool balls

3 lumps of coal (not good – unsure how to easily resolve the ensuing soot stains)

My favourite work top

All of the above were ultimately reclaimed through a fair exchange system of a treat per item, although, clearly sensing the increased desirability of the work top, this proved somewhat more costly to retrieve as he helpfully dragged it around the garden for an airing three times before feeling that it was suitable refreshed. I think my grandmother would have described this as building a rod for your own back but then I'm equally sure she didn't have a dog.

Saturday 27th May

The Chelsea Flower Show has to lot to answer for. Subtly teasing and tempting everyday gardeners across the land with microcosms of gardening utopia that could surely be conjured up in your own back yard with a simple swish of broom or a twist of fork. Unless that is, you happen to have a young puppy.

I say this because even the smallest job is just bloody difficult at the moment.

This dog is proving to be the worst possible gardener's companion.

I don't know what Monty Don did to get the sort of helpful sidekick I can only dream of, but in my case 'companion' is too generous a word. Radar is more like a gardening nemesis, constantly digging, pruning and fertilising in all the wrong places. All I was trying to do was plant *one* lavender bush. Just one. But this was extremely challenging. Admittedly, I probably shouldn't have committed the schoolgirl error of wearing gardening gloves, as the thrill of discovering that my hands suddenly possessed an additional layer that could be nipped, tugged off and played with was almost too much for him to resist. I tried to distract him with the gift of an old glove to play with - yes, I know that I'll pay for this later too and that this will challenge his ability to differentiate between permitted and forbidden gloves, but I was getting desperate. Throwing the old glove bought me a few seconds of planting time and finally, a little longer than it might otherwise have taken, the lavender was safely in position.

Which is why, despite the ongoing call of the wild, I have momentarily come in to write about his escapades instead.

Haha! As if! Stopped, mid-sentence by Radar running at a suspiciously fast pace from the lounge and out into the garden. A move that I now recognise as a clear indication of an item discovered and gleefully stolen, followed by an attempt to disappear with it before he is caught red-handed - or should that be red-pawed? Anyway, before I can escape any further into thoughts of appropriate idioms, I'm compelled to leap from my desk in hot pursuit, to discover that his treasure is a pencil - pretty much the only sharpened one easily available in the house – and now it is just four shards of shredded wood. He is a menace to writers and gardeners alike.

Luckily, I get an evening off tonight as we have been invited out to dinner with friends.

Well, almost an evening off. One minute after arriving, Sascha rings to say that the dog has leapt into the pond and proceeded to go completely mad, racing uncontrollably around the garden, showering everything in duck weed. This all sounds strangely familiar.

I remind her of the location of the spare towels and get handed a glass of wine.

Half-term Holiday

It turns out that Radar has a super-power. I'd heard about this before having a dog but not actually been witness to the amazing ability of a waggy, melty brown-eyed and silently sympathetic companion to soothe the pains of lost love. Sascha has just broken up with her boyfriend after a very intense few months together that saw him become seriously ill and thankfully recover. This alone, was enough of an emotional roller coaster, but romantic endings are especially brutal in the teenage years and Radar clearly realises he has a crucial role to play to that even as her mum, I cannot hope to do as effectively. He has spent the last couple of days sitting on her bed allowing endless hugs and listening without judgement to her misery and fury. I have to say that I am beginning to feel extremely grateful to Radar for his sympathy and good counsel as I'm pretty sure that any attempt at consolation from me would have been met much more brutally than with a simple stroke.

I think Sascha is slowly beginning to see chinks of light, but we are about to have to put this to the ultimate test. Tomorrow we are going away to Guernsey for four days without Radar, to attend a family wedding. Will the celebrations distract her or will the trauma of leaving the dog to go and witness the high point of someone else's romance prove too much to bear? This is unpleasantly nail-biting in more ways than one.

Following the state of the dog-sitter on our return from the last overnight trip, we decided to investigate alternative options. After checking out a few places we settled on a homestay in the next village. Radar had to be met and checked for sociability – a test that he passed with flying colours. Never has a dog been so amenable to meeting others – he'd rather roll on his back and stick his legs in the air than make an enemy. Good thing they didn't ask him to retrieve a ball or ignore a buttery plate left within reach – he'd have failed immediately.

Just to be on the safe side though, I have broken up the length of the homestay by asking my sister to collect him halfway through as they have a lovely dog-friendly home and an older dog to keep him company. I just hope this doesn't result in two sets of drawn and traumatised households when we get back. Or that he runs away never to be seen again. I have written detailed instructions describing all aspects of his routine and needs and am feeling like a nervous first-time mother. Again.

Four days later

Bizarrely, everything was OK. How could it be that all those doomsday scenarios I had conjured up didn't actually come to pass?

Or at least, not quite in the way I'd envisaged.

I learned, long after the event, that my sister did in fact lose the dog at one point, but she assures me that it was more a case of the dog losing them. Apparently, there is a subtle but crucial difference here: This was an entirely strategic move on their part, entailing hiding behind a bush whilst out on a walk. This game of hide and seek sufficiently spooked the dog to ensure he didn't dare stray from their side for the rest of his stay. Ingenious! This has done us a great favour as whilst Radar's recall still needs a little work, he certainly doesn't disappear too far in the wrong direction. What's more, he also behaved impeccably with Shuna, the new dog-sitter and she has assured us that he is welcome to return another time. Thank goodness – I don't think I could bear the nail-biting experience of yet another doggy boarding school selection test.

Tuesday June 7th

For some reason, it is indelibly etched in my memory that toddlers tend to reserve their very best tantrums and most piercing screams for busy public spaces. Supermarkets were my children's speciality, usually right next to an elderly and particularly noise-sensitive individual who would declare something equally unhelpful along the lines of 'Can't you shut that child up?' It was never a kindly one with slight hearing loss. It is the same with the dog.

I mean, obviously not *exactly* the same. He doesn't tend to let out piercing screams and I can't even begin to justify him supermarket entry under the guise of a support dog, but it turns out that he can throw an almighty strop.

This afternoon, he demonstrated his skills in this area by turning into a crazed monster in the middle of the village. This seems to have been brought on by a toxic combination of cold water after leaping into the stream, the use of the 5-metre extendable lead which I had forgotten sends him into a wild frenzy of semi-freedom, and my son's hysterical laughter. I, however, as the nominated focus of his frenzy, was not laughing as he leapt at me, wet and wild, looking to all intents and purposes as if he was ready to tear me apart, roll around with me on the ground and plunge us both into the water. Only by some miracle of dexterity and super-human power, did I managed to pin him down on the ground and undertake a lead change, before we turned on our tails (now well between our legs) and headed home - wet, muddy, but relatively unscathed.

Perhaps it was a one-off.

Sunday 12th June

Picture this. It is pouring with rain and still unreasonably early for a Sunday morning. I am standing in the garden in my pyjamas holding a watering can, slowly adding carefully positioned splashes to patches of grass.

Rest assured, I have not completely taken leave of my senses, though I am slightly nervous that any inquisitive neighbours who chance to open their curtains any time soon might think otherwise. As it happens, this is a totally justifiable activity intended to free the grass of the sticky remains of randomly placed piles of dog poo before someone unwittingly treads in it. Regrettably, a poo bag is sometimes not quite sufficient to fully retrieve the sloppiest excretions. I apologise if you're eating your breakfast, but I feel it's important to keep this real. Despite my best efforts, the lawn is still a minefield of shoe-sticking spreadable sh*t. I have not yet found a better way to avoid accidentally walking through this and bringing it inside, other than addressing the issue as soon as it happens and before the patches become lost to the casual observer in the depths of this grassy jungle. In practice, the torrential rain helps me to wash away the worst of it, but I have yet to properly explain my activity to any onlookers and can therefore only pray that the earliness of the hour is enough to protect me from being labelled as having completely lost the plot.

Friday 17th June.

Fox poo.

I had no idea that this was a thing until this-morning. Very naïve, I know, but there you go. For those fellow fortunates who have also unwittingly dodged the fox-related perils that a dog owner may have to contend with, I must share with you my learning for today: Fox poo is a BIG thing in the dog world and as such it will become part of yours too.

My awakening was impeccably timed. Having been spared the duty of the early morning walk, Doug returned from the field opposite just at the point that I stepped out of a long hot shower. I knew he had returned because in my dripping wet state he was desperately hollering for immediate assistance. Assuming a major emergency I grabbed a rather too flimsy (and not in the least absorbent) dressing gown (oh my how they cling when wet!) and raced down the stairs to be informed that the dog was covered in poo.

Fox poo.

Apparently, its smell is incontestable.

Actually, there was no 'apparently' about it.

By now (by which I mean about 10 seconds into our reacquaintance) I was fully versed in this new horror. Radar on the other hand was delighted to have discovered such a source of doggy elixir and had rolled in it so thoroughly that he would undoubtedly attract the attention of every fox fancier in Hampshire. Fearing an invasion of beagles or worse, not to mention the imminent threat of dispersal through the house, I set to with the hose, a washing-up bowl of water and some tea tree scented dog shampoo, thereby entirely negating the warm scented glow that I had just emerged from. In that regard alone, Radar and I had a lot in common and neither of us were in the least bit happy about it.

To gain some control over this new evil of dog ownership, I have been googling ways to avoid a repeat of this experience, revealing some promising results. Not least of these is the ultimate in foxy dog accessories – a fox poo coat! To be clear, this is not a dog coat made or scented with fox poo – that might just struggle on the sales front unless your dog has been trained in the art of online shopping. No, this is simply an easy to remove and washable dog coat for those hounds that love to roll in s**t.

Amazing – there is a whole world out there of unexplored dog solutions. What next?

Saturday 25th June

There is something very soothing about a summer's evening stroll and I have come to enjoy the relaxed feel of a short evening walk with no agenda other than a quick wee for the dog and a chance for me to walk off dinner in the fresh air. Except of course it doesn't always work quite like that when your companion is a bouncy half-trained boy who loves to stop everyone in their tracks and then demonstrate how friendly he is. Friendly of course, is somewhat open to interpretation and this-evening was no exception. I had barely got 30 metres from our front door when I bumped into one of the foremost gurus of impeccable dog behaviour that the village possesses. I had hoped that with Radar's urge to burn off the last bit of energy for the day, this meeting would amount to little more than a quick dog meet-and-greet session – a swift sniff of each other's bums and on we go, but no. Radar's compulsive friendliness translated into the perfect example of misbehaviour as he showed off his talent for leaping and jumping and twisting in a fit of over-excited glee rather than passing on by in a civilised manner. This was too much for the dog guru who was determined to support my inadequate efforts to regain control by turning our meeting into a full-on dog training session. She of course was perfectly equipped with tasty treats and a stern but determined manner that that put both me and my dog in our places as we were instructed on the 'correct manner' in which to greet politely rather than over-enthusiastically. Not daring to contradict her, we only just got away, 15 minutes later, without the dog completely losing the plot and having one of his crazy demon dog moments. For that at least I am grateful. We may never have been able to stroll the streets free of shame again if that had happened.

Free to wander once again, Radar enjoyed padding through the damp grass and muddy edges of the stream and so we extended our stroll with an unplanned loop past the village church.

This was a mistake.

Much to my horror, we found ourselves on a direct collision course with a wedding party dressed in all their finery. Traffic conditions made it impossible to step out into the road to avoid them. A toxic mix of unavoidable proximity, muddy paws, immaculate attire and a hyped-up dog. Forced to tough it out I grasped the lead with a firmness of grip and a sternness of voice that scary dog-guru lady would have been proud of and gripped the edge of the pavement with a clear and commanding 'LEAVE'. Reader, I can assure you that the wedding finery remained unsullied and what is more, such was the success of this manoeuvre, that I fooled the group into thinking I had a delightful and perfectly trained puppy with whom they were sorry not to be able to share a quick stroke. Fake it till you make it, as they say. And then make a sharp exit.

Friday 1st July

A hyper dog day. No listening at any point. Very grabby and nippy. Distinct lack of fun. Or at least I had no fun. Radar seemed perfectly happy with testing the boundaries of my tolerance.

Saturday 2nd July

It is not often that I envy anyone heading off to walk miles with a fully-laden backpack on an English summer's day with all the associated seasons of weather looking possible; but as Sascha headed off this-morning with Doug as chief taxi driver to do her Duke of Edinburgh expedition walk, I was unsure who had drawn the short straw. Still in recovery from yesterday's demoralising experience, there were no signs that Radar's compulsion to indulge in self-interested fun was waning.

By 8.00 am he had already shown the level to which he was prepared to put this expedition in jeopardy by:

- Running off and coating in saliva one off her hiking boots. (Had our chase instinct not been so finely tuned, I'm pretty sure it would have suffered serious chew damage within seconds).

- Stealing a favourite waterproof hat and discovering that with the right amount of nibbling, the rim was easily detachable.
- Absconding with the glue we were trying to use to fix the waterproof hat.
- Destroying a sandal. Yes, it was part of the expedition kit. Thank goodness it wasn't the boot.
- Snatching and then consuming all the goldfish food (no, not essential kit but no doubt a move designed to distract us from his next attempt on the backpack.)
- Eating half a giant cookie while I was trying to glue the hat.
- Remaining utterly oblivious to the rapidly increasing stress levels felt by my daughter who was not responding well to his attempts to counter all the days of meticulous planning that had gone into her preparations.

On this last count at least, I was quite glad when they were safely on their way with no irreparable damage.

It seemed that the best plan for the rest of the day was to actually do something fun with the dog, ideally with some support in tow; and so, remembering fondly how idyllic one of the local stretches of river always seemed for dogs and their owners, I invited my sister to join me for a hike to a beautiful stretch of the Test at Chilbolton, where we could stroll and he could paddle in the shallows if it took his fancy.

To make life easy, I thought it best to proceed on this walk with Radar on the lead, explaining to my sister that the thought of him racing bouncily towards a small child or greeting a dog-fearing adult were stressors that I just didn't feel we should test today. However, it was becoming clear that keeping him contained on the lead was not doing much to deplete his supreme energy levels and with plenty of other dogs freely playing in the water and wandering the meadows I finally agreed that in a quieter spot we could let him run free for a bit. Surely two adults and a bag of tasty treats to lure him back would be enough to maintain the upper hand?

You probably know where this is going by now.

Immediately after being granted his freedom, he runs up to what is very clearly to me, a fine example of a dog-hating man. Clinging momentarily to the hope that my instincts are blurred by nervous anticipation, I try not to overreact, but, in the process, evidently underreact as the dog's enthusiastic approach is greeted with a fierce declaration of 'Bloody dogs. GET OFF' and what looks like quite an aggressive shove of him out of the way with a walking pole. Now, I do get that some people don't like dogs and maybe I shouldn't have risked him off the lead, but Radar is hardly a vicious killing machine, just an over-friendly young dog. My maternal hackles were now fiercely raised and I ensured that as I recalled him and closely passed by the perpetrator, my eyes glowed a threatening shade of werewolf crimson.

Inside I was feeling far more tender.

We went back to plan A and continued around the outer edges of the water meadows with Radar kept firmly on the lead and away from the busier stretches. But we were not out of the woods yet. Just as we had put the first incident behind us, we were approached by a rather indignant couple who informed us that dogs were not allowed in this area at all. This time I was ready. There are, to be fair, regulations here about dogs running free in some areas, particularly during the nesting season as this is a Site of Special Scientific Interest, but I had done my research and was able to confidently confirm that we were allowed to walk here with him on the lead. Fortunately, this was enough to send them off muttering on their rather self-righteous path, but it doesn't make for a relaxing walk. I'm not someone who enjoys conflict – I'd much rather spread a little joy and a friendly hello. And that is one of the bigger challenges for me – having a dog can at times like this make you feel like a social leper or a parent with a particularly unruly child - you don't get to explain yourself, justify how hard you are trying or that your companion is perhaps not as bad as they may look superficially – you just get judged. The cute, universally adored puppy is now becoming the less publicly adorable boisterous child.

The day does end on a more soothing note as we take our evening stroll – from the back of The Old Vicarage the sounds of 1920's jazz gently flow across the village as a wedding party begins its evening vibe. Beautiful.

Sunday 3rd July

Sun. Coffee. Time sat doing nothing in garden with the dog resting his head quietly on my knee. All is well.

Perhaps Radar sensed I needed a break.

Tuesday 5th July

Today required precision planning. The main task was to get a carload of debris from a dismantled shower room taken to the dump and then to get the weekly shop done. This would require a good three hours of dedicated time and so the plan was to take the dog out for a long walk first thing and then get down to work while he slept it off.

So far, so good – the walk was achieved in good time, and it was looking as though we could proceed as planned.

Until he was sick.

And then he was sick again.

In fact, somehow, despite only having had one breakfast a couple of hours earlier, he managed a total of six bilious episodes before retreating to the sofa and looking thoroughly miserable.

The dump run is put on hold.

To add insult to injury, I'd also been hoping to take part in a friend's quiz night later but with the rest of the family having 'uncancellable' arrangements, the buck sits with me and the evening's big question will now be: How long will the dog's dinner stay down?

Radar perhaps felt a little guilty at having disarranged my evening and no sooner had I sacrificed my place on the quiz team he thoughtfully recovers sufficiently to snatch my newly hung bag of poo sacks from the coat stand and run around the garden refusing to relinquish them. This was vaguely reminiscent of the popcorn multipack he stole last week, where I was left chasing him as the contents slowly scattered in his wake, as I duly collected them in case he wolfed them down later and became sick. Feeling as though I'm going round in circles here in more ways than one.

For Radar however, this is clearly a very entertaining game with a deliciously nefarious twist - it provides your owner with a Russian roulette style experience as to whether the retrieved poo bags will survive fully intact or be pierced with small tooth-sized holes that will only be discernible after the bag has been filled with the contents of your bowels. Oh, to be a dog and have this much fun!

I think this might all be getting to me. My brain is trying to self-sooth with the rhythmical reassurance of childhood rhymes. In this case an adaptation in the style of Dr Seuss's Green Eggs and Ham:

I do not like this stupid game

I do not like it very much.

I do not like it in the house.

I would not like it with a mouse.

About the trail of poo bag sacks

I just don't give a flying ***k.

Would you risk them in your hand?

Would you fill one with contraband?

Not on my nelly.

Nor for a tickle on my belly.

I would not

Could not

Care a jot.

Ah - that's better. Nothing like a few rhyming couplets spat between gritted teeth to make you feel so much calmer. I shall order more poo bags.

Wednesday 6th July

The stairgate to the kitchen has broken. This is just up the dog's street. He can now enter this previously forbidden zone like a renegade cowboy entering the saloon, first crashing through the gate, then in a victorious finale, shooting straight for the main prize which is the kitchen swing bin. I suspect he's had this mission in mind for a few days and had somehow managed some act of masterful sabotage on the stairgate hinges since successfully sneaking in undetected a few days ago and absconding with the discarded remains of a very tasty lasagne. He could surely be the reincarnation of Butch Cassidy...come to think of it, maybe that explains his tolerance to hiding out in wait of steam trains...he must have been anticipating carriages packed with billions of golden lasagne slabs.

Friday 8th July

In my armoury of tools to conquer Radar's insatiable appetite for self-indulgent entertainment, I can now reliable identify his 'I've-stolen-something-I-shouldn't' run, that takes him out to the garden at a rapid pace intended to avoid capture or me spotting his misdemeanour. Ha! Thinks he can get the better of me, does he? Not a chance! He gives himself away at the first whisper of a run and today this was made even more obvious by the accompanying flash of pale blue that flashed across is speeding body. Totally unable to identify his quarry, I entered into rapid pursuit to discover that he had a trail of small smurfs hanging out of his mouth which were now being dragged ruthlessly across the lawn.

I have to admit to being completely perplexed.

Where did they come from? Smurfs were last seen in this house in 2010.

Monday 11th July

As a rare work-from-home treat, I get to join an hour of dog training over lunch. I'm hoping for great things and significant improvement and, to be fair, Radar seemed to be enjoying the class and showing some talent for the activities. The other trainee dog owners, however, are not having such a good time. Next to us is Sandy – a 6-month-old golden retriever whose owner tells me that his wife is ill and so he is having to stand in today. He looks quite nervous, though maybe he is just tired and hungry – apparently Sandy ate his entire cooked breakfast this-morning, apart from the fried egg, which he assumed was a little too warm for her liking. I find myself wondering whether Radar's enthusiasm for Sandy is him seeking a Goldilocks to roll with his inner cowboy...?

But there is no time for tea and sympathy and fairy tale musings. The activity for today's session is pocket training.

Or to be precise, 'pocket desensitisation'.

The idea behind this is to stop the dog from assuming that every time you put your hand in a pocket, it will emerge with a treat attached. I am a little alarmed by this concept as most of the obedience that I have been able to get out of him has been linked to the subtle - or maybe not so subtle, hand-to-pocket motion - undoing that seems totally counterproductive. Fortunately, very little progress was made as it seemed to me that every time the dog did what was expected and ignored the pocket, the owners were unable to stop themselves from rewarding this magnificent achievement with a treat fished straight out of a pocket. This was met with a good deal of frustration by the dog trainer, but a well-contained giggle and secret sigh of relief from me.

Time to get back to work.

Tuesday 12th July

Is there such a thing as post-puppy depression? I mean, I know I haven't talked about this very much until now, but there are some days when I just want to walk up that hill and cry. Having a puppy is a real rollercoaster ride and sometimes, when the house is a tip, work beckons, the kids keep shouting 'Mum' (rarely 'Dad' – why is that?) and no one else can be persuaded to hike up a hill in the rain with Radar, the responsibility of looking after him when I was the one who was initially the most reticent about taking on a puppy, brings me down.

And so, this-morning I am doing exactly that. Walking up a hill, on my own, trying not to cry. And failing abysmally. The pouring rain just adds to the drudgery, but at least lends a gratefully accepted disguise to my mood.

I am just so desperate to get some freedom but feel like the family dogsbody (unintended pun – but it has given me a momentary giggle). Even if someone came with me it would be nice, but Doug still struggles with energy and back pain and so very often I'm simply trying to relieve the pressure from him. The kids are great on a sunny day but nagging really doesn't add to the fun. Oh, and I almost forgot to mention that today Radar is looking a little off colour. In fact, Doug thought he looked a bit depressed and off his food and suggested we speak to the vet.

This is an inspired suggestion and I praise him enthusiastically for it and give him a treat. OK, I don't. Might be just a bit patronizing, but I can admit to being sorely tempted. Recalling the vet's comforting presence and reassuring accent, I feel that I will unquestionably also benefit from a visit. Radar and I head off together.

It's a good thing we have a very tolerant vet as I do sometimes feel like an over-anxious and protective parent, but he kindly suggested that the slight cough might be kennel cough or lung worm or possibly just hay fever, but to be on the safe side, recommended a course of antibiotics and no further dog contact for a week. He also helpfully points out that the incubation period for kennel cough can be over five days and so immediately I find myself thinking about how only yesterday, Radar was happily licking the chops of my friends blonde Alsatian...he really does seem to have a thing for blondes. Will I now have to mention this to them (the kennel cough that is, not the blonde obsession) and hope that we don't become outcasts of local dog society? What are the guidelines on publicly sharing potential contamination with a highly infectious respiratory virus? Radar just stares knowingly as if the answer is obvious. I have no idea what he is trying to tell me.

Thursday 14th July

The storm has passed and summer has returned. There is nothing for it but to throw my newly purchased tropical print picnic banket across the lawn the moment I get home from work and just soak in some late afternoon rays. The dog soon chooses to join me. Gently licking my hair (do I smell of fox poo or bacon?), prodding me with his paw, moulting all over the mat and then sharing a blast of poo-scented aerosol as the wind shifts in my direction.

Friday 15th July

Friday afternoons are always a weak point in managing to hold things together at the best of times but incorporating Radar into our plans adds an extra layer to the fun.

Basically, we were, as usual running late to get to Charlie's piano lesson. This was partly because he was proudly reading his school report to my mother-in-law and partly because just at the very moment that we made it out of the front door, Radar decided to make an unexpected bid for freedom, running towards the road rather than into the car, having not heard the bit about needing to drop off at piano *before* going on a walk. Charlie had casually popped back inside to get himself a drink whilst I dropped everything and ran to retrieve Radar, narrowly grabbing his collar before he could get himself into any danger. Slightly shocked but relieved to get dog and son safely into the car, we head off.

It is only as we get to the piano teacher's house that I realise, with mounting horror, that my purse, phone and current read (Kate Humble's 'Friend for Life'- I'm not appreciating the irony of this at the moment) are not in the car. I know that I brought them out of the house because I had to drop them to free my hands to grab the absconding dog. The scene flashes back before my eyes and I now see what came to pass: The valuables were placed on the roof of my car and in my rush to bundle everyone in, I completely forgot about them. With mounting horror, I can now picture them scattered and fatally crushed somewhere in the country lanes behind me. I dump the boy and retrace my drive.

Nothing.

Sascha offers to take Radar and scour the village as I return to pick up Charlie and check the route again.

Still nothing.

And then, there is a glimmer of hope.

Many months ago, we set up some sort of tracking device on our phones so that we could locate them if lost and after some technical issues with accessing this we discover that according to the app, my phone is currently about 10 miles away in another village entirely.

And then it is on the move...

It seems to be making a very peculiar journey, full of short stops and starts in what appeared to be a giant circle around Winchester.

Just at the point that I concluded I should be cancelling all my cards and finding a way to remotely wipe my phone memory - no, I hadn't got round to setting up password protected access - we notice that the phone appears to have made its way to Winchester police station.

Moments later, I get a call on the landline. Silently thanking my lucky stars that I still have one of these, a Police Officer tells me that all three items were spotted flying from the roof of my car by an Iceland delivery driver who had just dropped them into her at the station at the end of his shift. Immensely relieved, we head straight to the station to collect everything before closure, eternally grateful to the delivery driver who even tried, despite speaking limited English, to ring a friend of mine whose number he found in my purse. What a star!

Sunday 17th July

BREAKING NEWS - Radar has learned to swim!

Swimming might not seem *that* ground-breaking for a Labrador. Surely with their ancestors stretching in a direct line to the heroic sidekicks of many a Canadian fisherman, a gentle Hampshire stream would be something that a Labrador should embrace without a backwards glance.

Not so.

Radar has been pathetically tentative about getting much more than his paw pads wet until now and so needed some gentle encouragement. Emboldened by a hot and sticky walk to the river, Sascha and I valiantly waded into the river with him, gradually venturing deeper until it was almost inevitably swimming depth for Radar. Sensing the depth of his predicament, his pace of advance slowed to a stubborn stop and an anxious shadow crossed his face, somewhat akin to the drama that you might expect at the peak of a Shakespearian tragedy. He was weighing up his options: Was it riskier to advance further and ultimately reach the other side or risk a doggy paddle back to the bank? It seemed pointless to reason with the dog that he was not dangerously dipped, in the style of Macbeth, on the verge of a treacherous blood bath; but rather, was plunged in a crystal-clear chalk stream with two loving bodyguards who'd risk their life for him.

But he wasn't taking any chances.

Uncertain as to his fate, he sensibly attempted to leap into our arms rather than risk his own demise, before suddenly discovering with great joy that it was all much ado about nothing and HE COULD DOGGY-PADDLE!

Such a courageous and talented dog! We couldn't have been prouder! Or wetter.

Friday 22nd July

The end of term has finally arrived leaving me delirious with excitement and relief. So much so, that with the additional delirium brought on by a surprisingly hot evening, I spontaneously decided that we needed to replace our patio furniture. The last table was so rickety that it was now a serious health and safety risk along with four chairs that presented similar levels of danger to anyone brave enough to sit on them and it was looking like we were going to be spending a lot of time this summer sitting in the garden no matter what the weather, throwing balls for the dog.

Not having the patience to hold back and wait for weeks once a decision like this is made, we headed straight to the garden centre and three hours later a van delivered a six-seater table with parasol and spinning central lazy Susan, thereby effectively putting the kibosh on a summer of indulgent BBQ gatherings and long hot nights.

There is just one thing that I didn't consider in my It's-the-holidays-and-the-sun-is-out-and-I-don't-care-about-the-cost moment of carefree euphoria, and that was whether a wicker style patio suite would withstand the chewy jaws of the dog.

In a moment of panic at this realisation, I carried out a closer inspection of the chewability of the chairs. Not a practical test – the term wasn't quite bad enough to send me to my knees ready to bite the nearest chair leg – just a simple visual once over. It seems to be made from a sort of weather-resistant plasticky wicker look-alike material. I pray that this is as resistant to shredding by sharp juvenile dog teeth as solid wood. Oh dear... will we live to regret the sensible ordinariness of the solid wood designs or the unchewable but rather uncomfortable aluminium sets? I have no idea, but for now I am fiercely guarding every chewable chair leg with my life, feeling life I'm living through some sort of dystopian party game of musical chairs, but without the party. This is proving unexpectedly challenging as there are six chairs, each offering the requisite four legs. It doesn't take a mathematician to picture how entertaining this game could become.

Saturday 23rd July

If anything should strike fear into the hearts of dog owners across the land it has to be this:

THE DOG WARDEN.

In the hierarchy of **Wardens to Dread**, the dog warden is the ~~pinnacle~~ top dog. Far worse than the car park stalking traffic warden leaving conspicuously coloured car stickers as his calling card, or even a prison warden overseeing their inmates. No, the Dog Warden's reach stretches way beyond the prison or car park walls and into the dark back streets beside your home, waiting and ready to grab your pooch and whisk him to the pound never to be seen again if he ever dares to venture alone beyond his walls.

Ok - not quite true. In fact, not true at all – those childhood tales have a lot to answer for. Dog wardens of the real world do a fantastic job of promoting responsible dog ownership and helping strays find a bed for the night and beyond. But hey, I was secretly enjoying adding a dystopian sense of drama to the events of the day which really did involve a nerve-wrackingly narrow miss with a real-life Dog Warden.

It all started with the news that a spaniel had been found wandering around the village on his own yesterday afternoon, and, despite most local dogs being more reliably on first name terms with the rest of the community than their owners, no one could identify who this one belonged to. The news of the lost dog raced across social media in a desperate attempt to locate his owners but for hours he remained unclaimed. The community could do nothing but get him to the vets and see if he had an identity chip. We waited, phones in hands waiting for the ping of a happy ending.

But then the news took a turn for the worse – his microchip was OUT OF DATE and he was going to have to be passed on to the dog warden.

The only hope was that the owners would hear of his predicament and claim him before he risked being rehomed alone, miles from all his loving friends and family. Sorry, veering into the dramatic again, but it did have me mentally checking that that Radar's chip was fully functional.

Fortunately, after 24 hours of neighbourhood nail-biting, technology came to the rescue as dog and owner were reunited, thanks to a well-shared Facebook post. Phew!

Sunday 24th July

For once, the walk to the River with Radar was perfectly timed – the water was teaming with friendly-looking dogs and there was not a small child in sight – just a few stone skimming teenagers who were easily avoided by a short paddle downstream. I breathed a sigh of relief at not having to choose between holding him back from his new-found love of water or risk him bouncing over-enthusiastically towards a toddler. We were free to let him loose!

Radar immediately found himself another blonde he liked the look of – this time in the form of a golden Labrador, and I slipped into one of those conversations with her owner that happen so naturally between dog owners who find themselves knee deep in the same patch of river. Turns out she has five teenagers at home and finds that the great upside to having a dog is that at least one member of the family greets you with enthusiasm when you walk through the door home, and without the slightest bit of backchat. She makes a valid point. Sometimes these little reminders of how lucky we are to have a dog are all the boost I need.

Monday 25th July

Time for our first family outing to the seaside with Radar in tow! Yet again, my middle-aged brain is plying me with ginger beer-fuelled fantasies of picnics and paddling on the beach with our heroic and faithful hound by our side, ready to rescue a ….

Hang on…Sorry. …Really must stop this. It's not the 1950's anymore. In fact, it wasn't even the 1950's when I was a child, and we never took our dog to the beach; but we didn't have social media to brainwash us when I was a child and so we just had to make do with Blyton…but that's by the by.

Here we are, knee-deep in the 21st century, and we haven't even left the house before we hit a snag. It turns out, that at this time of year, the melting pot of beach-dog-picnics is a dangerous mix and one that I have no desire to experiment with. But finding a dog-friendly beach is not straightforward. Devoid of a sea-stained treasure map to draw us towards the perfect beach, we resorted to an internet surf and duly followed the ~~stars sun~~ satnav. We were back in the game.

Starting with a walk along the cliff tops, we wound our way down to the shore where Radar declared himself the first to 'See the Sea' racing to the cliff edge with us in hot pursuit. Screeching to a halt at the sight of this infinite pond he appeared equally tempted and terrified at the prospect of wading in. It wasn't quite the gently flowing experience he'd tested his sea (river?) legs on last weekend, and much to his disgust, he also quickly discovered that it was utterly undrinkable. And then there were the waves to contend with - one moment you think you've got the whole depth thing under control, and then the next moment you're up to your neck and being pushed off your paws. Still, it didn't seem to put him off and with long stretches of empty beach to run and dry off along, it was soon time to head of the beach café for lunch.

This wasn't quite the carefree picnic lunch I'd been envisaging as, well, to be honest, we hadn't got round to packing a picnic in amongst the dog treats, towels, collapsible water bowl and collection of leads. So, the beach café it was. Fortunately, sitting obediently next to us waiting to be fed treats and the occasional chip, was a task that Radar felt was within his remit for the day and *so* admirably did he perform this role, that within a few minutes a young girl couldn't resist coming up and asking to stroke him. Radar obligingly rolled onto his back, delighted to be so adored.

A little too delighted as it turns out.

Concerned at the sudden retreat of the girl as Radar lay there looking like he was the happiest dog on the planet, we noticed that he had become a little overstimulated - his willy was now protruding very obviously for all to see, much to the horror of his new admirer.

I tried to act as if this was nothing to be embarrassed about but couldn't help but inwardly cringe on her behalf and was only grateful that Radar appeared completely ignorant of the physical manifestations of his delight.

Tuesday 26th July

This has not been a great dog day.

Radar's behaviour is really getting me down and I cannot understand why he saves the worst of it for me. Frustratingly, it is the evening walks through the village, which I would normally enjoy so much, that are proving the most demoralising. For no apparent reason he has taken to repeatedly jumping at the lead and grabbing at my hand with his mouth in what feels like quite an aggressive game. Except, as much as he might think it's a game, I *really* don't and feel as though I am going to get badly hurt by this if it carries on. If I try telling him off firmly, he momentarily turns away and even submissively rolls on his back, but moments later, leaps back up as if all is forgiven and is starts it all again. This is not just humiliating, as he chooses to perform this charade anywhere with a decent audience, but I'm also terrified that he might get a reputation as being an aggressive dog. How firm I should be with him? With the children I have always tried to be calm and controlled when their behaviour is bad, but perhaps with dogs the approach needs to be fierce and more dominant? But will this make things worse? Can I even bear to add to the whole embarrassing experience and be obliged to act out the role of an aggressive dog-mother in front of all the goody-goody four paws looking on at this imperfect pantomime? I know that sometimes things need to get worse before they get better, but this is far from what I pictured pre-dog, when I naively imagined that walks and time together would be what would make it all worthwhile.

My misery must have been clear on my return home as Doug offers to accompany me on our next walk to see what's going on. This is a rare event as I usually walk alone to save him from having to push himself too much, but I'm getting desperate. Part of me wonders whether Radar will dare put on a performance with both of us present, but I needn't have concerned myself on that front. The leaping and grabbing started even before we had left the driveway and continued at regular intervals. And so, our rare walk as a couple was punctuated by practising dominating the dog and giving clear commands with full eye contact. Apparently, I should also be talking to the dog more and including training sessions in my walk to remind him who is in control. Marvellous. Now even the pleasure of a casual stroll is pie in the sky.

Wednesday 27th July

Another dog day dawns, and with it a flimsy but flickering flame of hope for a better day rises from the embers of yesterday's burn out.

Rested and emboldened, I decided to get straight back out and test drive the techniques we talked through yesterday for mastering my dog's crazy behaviour. I could pretend that this determined approach was all down to inner strength and a refusal to accept defeat, but this would be a lie. The truth is that as of tomorrow, Radar will be on vacation with Shuna, his new favourite dog sitter as we are off to Spain for a few days. The thought of leaving her with a badly behaved dog is just as worrying as telling her of his errant ways and risk having to cancel the holiday and so I've been frantically trying to come up with a backup plan all week. Just as my dilemma grew increasingly bothersome and with no obvious solution in sight, I was saved by the closest thing I have to a fairy ~~god~~ dogmother: Shuna, the dog-sitter herself, who appeared as if by magic as we were out walking.

"...I'm having a few problems with his behaviour" I

spluttered in an attempt to get the confession over and done with as quickly as possible.

I waited for the inevitable.

Any moment now she was going to ban him for life from her dog haven.

But something unexpected was happening...

As I stared shamedly down at my shoes, Radar, eavesdropping intently, sat impeccably at my heels and gazed adoringly up into her eyes.

"Oh, I think we can handle that" replies Shuna with an air of being remarkably unphased. "That is typical of dog of his age."

...Really?

Can it be true that I am not actually entirely alone in this dystopian version of dog ownership and that maybe, just *maybe*, he will move through this phase?

Ears fully pricked, Radar sat by my feet, clearly perfectly satisfied with the direction the conversation was taking. He might have fooled Shuna, or maybe he just prefers staying there and this is all a great ruse to hang out in dog heaven surrounded by a gang of playful canine pals?

Who knows, but my relief was palpable. If I'd been of Radar's mindset, I'd probably have chosen this moment to leap around her showing my teeth in a friendly doggy grin or perhaps just rolled on my back and let her tickle my tummy. Thankfully I'm not that in tune with him as such a scenario would have done nothing to counter the stage show that Radar was already forcing us to star in. For now, I just need to practice getting this under control.

Thoughtfully, Radar provides me with multiple opportunities to work on my domination technique with a battle plan worthy of a great general. He starts by lulling me into a warm self-satisfied glow with a pleasant trot to the village centre, as I engage him in conversation about the weather and what a good boy he is, sharing the occasional treat in celebration of his brilliance. Well, I share, and he takes, but let's not split hairs over this.

Three hundred metres are travelled without incident. And then we reach the centre stage, where, at the sight of a perfect audience in the form of two fellow dog owners (far more experienced types with well-behaved companions), Radar leaps into action. Once again, I'm subjected to a game of pseudo-attack and try to firmly put him in his place without losing any more ground. The audience stand observing the battle from the safety of the side-lines and, as we appear to reach a momentary ceasefire, they bravely approach to offer comment on the situation. Their suggestion is that I could deal with this rather 'interesting' behaviour (I accept this choice of adjective gracefully, whilst inwardly acknowledging its extreme generosity) by attending square bashing sessions with him – something that has apparently 'worked wonders for a couple with a troublesome pup down the road'.

I have absolutely no idea what they are referring to. My understanding of square bashing was some sort of repetitive military marching drill. I promise to look into it, whilst crossing my fingers tightly behind my back – there is *no* way I'm becoming the dog-owner equivalent of a drill sergeant. We part ways with a smile as they reassure me that Labradors can be notoriously difficult to train, but that they are usually better by the age of four. I smile gratefully, but inside I'm screaming like an overwrought toddler. FOUR YEARS? I have no idea what state I'll be in if I must endure four more years like this.

Eventually we make it home, though not without repeated episodes at key locations. On the upside, I got to practice publicly asserting myself whilst trying to hold a polite conversation at least twice more, and then, just as I'm beginning to feel as though I've been tested sufficiently for one outing, we have a glimmer of a breakthrough. Radar shows the first signs of thinking about launching an attack and then stops himself, as if thinking better of it. I leap on this moment with as much praise and delight as I can muster and promptly race home before he could have a change of heart. This moment of magnificent self-control on behalf of the dog was of course a private one – he is a dog of modest character and had no need to show-off his genius to the general public.

Thursday 28th July

The house is eerily quiet.

Radar has been dropped off for his holiday having barely given us a backwards glance as he raced off to run around Shuna in over-excited circles and then play with the other dogs.

We, however, are immediately noticing his absence. I hadn't realised how aware I was of his every move or the extent to which I'd developed a nervous vigilance every time that I walk out of the kitchen or leave a room - I am constantly on my guard against what mischief he might be getting up to every time my back is turned. And yet, I am secretly breathing a sigh of relief. This is the first time in nearly five months that I have been able to freely hoover up his endlessly moulting dog hair without it being immediately replaced with more.

If anyone ever tries to tell you that a Labrador only moults for a few days, twice a year, DO NOT believe them. The reality is that they shed hair continuously and at times, in extremis. In fact, should you ever find yourself needing to enlighten any doubters or deniers out there, it might be advisable to empty your hoover bag weekly on their hair-free carpets just to prove a point. Jump on it and kick it around the place if you want. This sort of public information should not be pushed under the carpet.

Turns out that I really should have remembered what a hassle karma can be before suggesting the hoover bag strategy...

Just as I was really beginning to get some long overdue satisfaction from all that sucking (of hair up the hoover in case that wasn't clear), I notice that the diamond in my engagement ring has fallen out. My heart skips a beat as I rewind the day's activities. I have been running around packing, tidying, dog walking and yes, hoovering, for hours. It could be anywhere. Panic is setting in and the situation is clearly going to require immediate back-up. Within minutes, the whole family are on their hands and knees and crawling around the house. Nothing. The hoover gets emptied and its hairy contents strewn across the floor to be gone through with a fine-tooth comb. Still nothing. We check the driveway, the half-packed suitcases and even the grass. Zilch.

Really feeling the karmic payback at this point.

And then, just as I'm building up to a dangerous rant against the dog, diamond and domestic drudgery that are sabotaging the start of our holiday, I decide to crawl around on the dining room floor and by way of a small miracle, spot the missing gem glistening under the radiator. I take this as a message to put the hoover away, start re-packing and get the hell out of here.

Saturday 30th July

If you think that leaving the country and flying hundreds of miles south is enough to step away entirely from thoughts of your fur baby*, then I should gently point out that we are currently failing abysmally. Whilst I cannot deny that having the luxury of a genuine lie-in is heavenly, the level of relaxation that staying in a scorching rural corner of Southern Spain with no imperative but to eat, drink and admire the view has led me to suggest a family art activity. Inspired by a recent trip to an exhibition of coloured pencil drawings, today we are all going to create an image of the dog. There was surprisingly good take up on this suggestion. Maybe everyone is missing him, or perhaps the non-existent internet is a factor, but either way we are all devoting ourselves to creating Radar masterpieces. Charlie finishes his in half an hour. Doug looks as though he is creating something worthy of The National Gallery, Sascha doesn't want to reveal hers until it is perfect but is looking put out by the boys' efforts, and I am cheating by printing out a photo in cartoon style format that I will then just have to colour in. Art never was my strong point. I have no idea why I suggested this activity. Must be down to the midday sun and the lack of mad dogs to keep me on the right track.

*Oops I did it again. Last time. Really.

Thursday 4th August

After a few days of radio silence from the dog haven, I send a rather overdue text to Shuna today to check that everything is going smoothly. With only two days to go before we are reunited, I sense that it is time to prepare myself for whatever mischief he might have got up to in our absence and to suss out whether we will ever be able to go on holiday without him again or whether we should remain in Spain and go on the run.

The response is not quite what I had been bracing myself for. In glowing tones, Shuna replies by profusely extolling Radar's virtues and saying that he is growing into a lovely dog. But…(isn't there always a but?) we might like to be aware that he is showing a very strong interest in the girls. She proceeds to attach some photographic evidence of Radar lying on the sofa with his legs in the air, fast asleep after having exhausted himself chasing his favourite new 'friend' – a cockpit - I *really* didn't make this up. Her name is Bonny. Of course it is.

Ah.

Well. That's great. We haven't even had to deal with this with the kids yet. I can't decide whether to be grateful for that or not.

Sunday 7th August

We returned home last night to an exhausted dog, who clearly thought he was still dreaming when we came in to wake him up this-morning. Reassuringly, he almost seemed pleased to see us. Could it be possible that he has had just a bit too much of a good thing?

Wednesday 10th August

There is a bag of dog sick in my fridge.

Before you question this, rest assured that it is just as easily explained away as my early morning adventure with a watering can in the pouring rain.

Today had been an early start for the rest of the household. So early, that they had managed to feed the dog, take him for a quick walk and leave the house in such a state of bleary-eyed blindness, that they hadn't noticed the yellow pile of regurgitated gunk that Radar had left on the dining room floor overnight. Or maybe that's exactly why they left so promptly?

On closer investigation - an unfortunate side-effect of having to clear it up - the vomit turns out to be a bizarre mix of shards of sharp wood, large beans and a small dishcloth. Where on earth had he even found this weird mix of stuff and why would you choose to eat it even if you are a

Labrador?

Half panicked by the thought that this might represent some sort of medical emergency whilst also eager to remove this repulsive concoction from my floor, I felt that I needed a second opinion. With no one due home for an hour or so, I concluded that the only thing to do was to bag up the mess to show them when they got back. But where to put it? The bin was out as studying a bag of sick is bad enough without having to retrieve it first from a fetid pile of potato peelings. Left on the side, it would stink the room out and I really didn't want to look at it. The freezer would make investigation impossible, so, the fridge it was. Totally justifiably. Obviously.

On their return, I immediately offer up the chance to study the sick bag in the fridge, but this is robustly declined with a rapid flurry of offers to 'keep an eye on the dog' and 'see how he goes'.

Admittedly, Radar seems totally fine. I resign myself to the prospect of feeling obliged to study his next few bowel movements and general demeanour for a day or so and hastily remove the bag to the dustbin.

Saturday 13th August.

The dog holiday.

This feels very indulgent, having just come back

from a few days away in Spain, but back in March, before we could even imagine being able to leave the country without him for a holiday, we had hedged our bets and booked a dog holiday to Devon.

And what would an account of a first year with a dog be worth if it didn't involve a road trip to an idyllic dog-friendly cottage in the height of the holiday season?

As far as Radar is concerned, the day has started very badly. The sight of suitcases being packed has sent him into a depressive state and he is lying with a miserable look on his face in an armchair in the lounge, refusing to engage as we pack all his worldly possessions into the car.

I try to explain that we are not abandoning him to another week of chasing anything that moves at the dog sitters, although why he wouldn't fancy that is anybody's guess. Nor are we planning on rehoming him for partaking in incessant theft and criminal damage; but this falls on deaf ears, wrapped firmly flat against his head. That is until all the packing is done and we are ready to head off, at which point he enthusiastically leaps from his throne with a stretch and a wag and jumps into the car.

Road trips turn out to be something that Radar was born for. Not once, on the whole journey did he ask if we were nearly there, bicker nastily or complain about the choice of music.

The same cannot be said for the rest of the family.

One hour into the journey and it becomes apparent that we hadn't yet slipped into the chilled-out holiday vibe. It had seemed like a good idea to stop for a rest break just off the A303 at Mere – we could park up, use the toilets, take the dog for a short walk and a wee, maybe even grab a coffee for the road. It was a perfect best-laid plan.

Until the dog unexpectedly yelps.

Doug, somewhat ill advisedly, blamed this on Sascha, who being a very experienced and archetypal teenager, took this so dramatically to heart that she stormed off and implemented immediate radio silence.

This whole scene played out in the two minutes that I had taken to visit the public toilets.

Half an hour passed trying to decode exactly what had happened and having our calls and texts ignored until finally, she returned, announcing that she had decided to climb a hill. Radar greets her particularly enthusiastically, perhaps hoping that she'll do it again and take him with her. For his sake, if not ours, she concedes that she may be able to continue the journey with her intolerable parents and sibling. It dawns on me that this could be why families need dogs as a silent, forgiving friend on hand when ever required. Radar blinked at me knowingly and I reply with a grateful wink.

We are definitely on the same page.

I attempted to mirror his inner calm, reminding myself that families across the land are enjoying similar starts to the holidays with their beloved teenagers and tried to feel gratitude for the fact that our prolonged break did at least give me the chance to get a decent coffee. Just had to pray that none of us needed to stop for a wee again too soon.

As is turned out, the rest of the journey proceeded without significant mishap, and we even arrived in time to walk down to the beach and enjoy an evening dip in the sea. The house was perfect and so far, everything remains intact apart from a football that Radar discovered with a little too much enthusiasm in the garden. It is now punctured and partially shredded and relegated to the dustbin. I can only live in hope that this is the limit of any dog-induced damage this week.

Sunday 14th August

It is always dangerous when you relax enough to step back and revel in how well-behaved and adaptable your dog is on his first proper holiday. Not that I would discourage these moments of indulgence – they can be just the boost you need for when, just around the corner, your illusions are thrown into the air and land with a nasty bump.

Today was a case in point.

So focussed were we on the fate of the football yesterday evening, that as dusk settled on our first evening, we had failed to notice a gently trickling, but rather muddy stream, flowing across the far edge of the garden. Lulled into a gentle sense of security, we sat enjoying the first coffee of the morning, relaxing to thoughts of how easy (burst balls aside) a dog holiday was proving to be. Radar had slept through the night in the kitchen with barely a whimper, enjoyed a good breakfast and was currently enjoying sniffing the view across the lawn and down to the sea.

Suitably tranquilised by this idyllic scene, I wandered into the kitchen to grab a second cup. This was also the moment that Radar picked to leap into the shallow stream for a bracing morning dip, and then race in from the garden to announce his delight at this unexpected treat by leaping onto our bed of beautifully clean, crisp white sheets. Why he had saved his first leap onto a human bed to coincide with being caked in wet mud is something he refuses to be drawn on.

I gave up on the idea of a second coffee to strip the bed and put on a wash.

On a more positive note, Radar was now perfectly clean having wiped his paws very effectively on the linen.

Monday 16th August

Taking a dog on holiday, especially one that is young and has barely explored the world beyond his own village is a massive learning curve. For us and the dog.

For the more obvious challenges we were suitably braced and had tried to put plans in place:

- Would he travel well in the car? Tick
- Pitstops prepared in advance? Tick
- Was the garden secure? Tick
- Dog-friendly beach within walking distance? Tick
- Dog-friendly pubs nearby? Tick

Clearly, we'd thought of everything.

So today, safe in the knowledge that we had all our bases covered, we decided to head into Salcombe. Radar approached this adventure with typically high levels of enthusiasm – he sprang along the crowded slipway to the East Portlemouth ferry like a film star trying to forge his way through throngs of adoring fans before leaping onto the boat to sail away into the sunset with barely a backwards glance. Well, ok, the sun wasn't setting, and not everyone was as delighted to meet him as he was, but Radar remained oblivious and just cruised on regardless.

If nothing else, it seemed clear at this point, that our dog had the most magnificent sea legs. Yet more irrefutable evidence of generations of breeding from his origins as a working sea dog.

We were feeling very proud that he was proving so true to this heritage and secretly smug that we hadn't chosen a pug.

So smug in fact, that rather than limit ourselves to that two minute crossing, we thought it would be lovely to go take him on an hours-long estuary cruise. All our fellow passengers appeared to be dog-lovers and greeted him with typically indulgent smiles and strokes. Everyone that is, apart from one non-English speaking Japanese tourist whose body language shrieked volumes as she secured her position at a safe distance from our motley crew at the far end of the boat. It wasn't long though, before I was wondering if she was possibly the most dog-savvy among us, as within moments of casting off, Radar started to emit some very worrying sounds from the depths of his stomach and bowels. Envious of her position at a safe distance from his rear end, I was sorely tempted to join her, but Radar had sat on my feet, pinning me firmly in my place. The gentleness of the offshore breeze did nothing to waft away the increasingly pongy evidence that we might be on the brink of a toileting disaster at sea. Visions of an emergency evacuation by life raft in the event of the air aboard becoming unbreathable, flash before my eyes. There was nothing to do but hope and pray that we would make it back to shore before we and our fetid dog were thrown overboard.

Learning point: *Ensure thorough evacuation of dog's bowels before boarding any form of inescapable public transport.*

Having held our breath for the longest hour of my life, we miraculously made it back to shore without incident and gasp a collective deep sigh of relief. That is, all of us except Radar. Whilst we might have been ready to kiss the ground, as far as Radar was concerned, things had suddenly got an awful lot worse. The pontoon that we had disembarked onto was gently swaying under his paws. Under the metal grating, water rolled unpredictably. This was not the solidity of dry land that he had been anticipating and so he stood, a terrified and quivering wreck, refusing to move in any direction. Torn between concern over the delicate state of his stomach and the urgent need to bribe him to move, we resorted to the latter, eventually making it to the shore after he had consumed a large quantity of treats and a mini chew bone. Perhaps he wasn't such a sea dog after all...

Learning point: *Pugs would be more portable in the event of a refusal to move on a wobbly surface.*

We decide to take a stroll through the quieter part of town to ease our nerves and reassure Radar that he was safely back on solid ground and so wind our way towards the parish church where a book fair is underway. Unable to resist a quick browse I leave them stretching the dog's legs whilst I head inside.

I got as far as the church porch before I hear them hail from the other side of the graveyard. Charlie comes running to tell me that Radar has weed on one grave and pooed on another. Why do I need to be informed of this? Can't they deal with it quietly rather than alerting the whole of Salcombe? I hand over another poo bag and head inside to claim sanctuary. There's no time limit on this is there? Pretty sure I could hang out in here for at least a day or so?

I lasted three minutes.

Wednesday 18th August

Having realised the errors of our ways yesterday in terms of correctly preparing to use public transport with your canine companion, we decided that we were ready to put this learning to the test by trying out a trip on a bus. Just a short ride to start with, from a Park and Ride on the edge of Plymouth into the town centre where we could explore the seafront and the port before heading back home.

The bus ride went incredibly smoothly. Quick wee in the carpark before boarding and then he sat quietly by our feet doing a marvellous impression of a well-trained guide dog. He kept up this charade until it was time to disembark. But then came the rub. Having been so focussed on the transport logistics, we hadn't put much thought to the challenges of bringing a country raised dog, more used to meeting little more than the odd walker or perhaps a runner, into the centre of a bustling city at the height of summer.

The next couple of hours were not so straightforward.

Every metre we travelled seemed to require him to mark his territory over the scent of the previous thousand dogs that had passed that way. And then when there could surely be no more wee left in him, there were plentiful cigarette buts and discarded food wrappings to investigate. Progress was painfully slow and by now it was midday with the sun was beating down hard. Normally, this would be an absolute gift – below us the Plymouth lido had never looked so tempting for a cooling dip -a sparkling semi-circle of refreshing aquamarine overlooking the ocean. But this was not an option for us with a dog in tow. Radar accepted this with grace, cooling off with a quick dip in the sea off the rocks, while we melted, clinging precariously to the slippery terrain and gripping his lead as he bounced and splashed delightedly in the water. The mood among the teenage members of our pack dipped dramatically. A couple of placatory ice creams later and we felt that we'd tested our mettle enough and headed back to the countryside.

Learning point: *You can take the dog into the city, but you can't put the city into the dog.*

Thursday 19th August

Low point:

Walking along the coastal path to visit a lighthouse, hands tucked deep into my pockets against the cool breeze and smatterings of rain that hit in stark contrast to yesterday's heatwave. Comfortingly, there is a cosy softness to the inside of my pockets that I couldn't quite discern. I squash it gently, momentarily grateful for its squidgy warmth, before a nauseating reality dawns.

This is the bag of dog poo I'd stashed there minutes earlier.

Do other people have this problem? What do you do when there isn't a bin in sight and hanging a plastic poo bag by the side of a narrow cliff-edge path for every passer-by to admire seems inappropriate?

Anyway, there it was in my pocket, and despite the double bagging I was becoming very aware that it *really* stank, cruelly forcing me to suffer the indignity of wafting said odour at anyone who passed me. Worse than that, the rest of the family had wandered slightly ahead with the dog (I can hardly blame them) and so I didn't even had the presence of Radar to explain away my unfortunate aroma.

By the time we had returned to the car the situation was becoming critical. Facing the possibility of having to drive home with the stinky sack doing its worst in the confines of the car, inspiration struck in the form of an extra-large disposable Costa coffee cup. Bingo! With its sealable lid this would surely make the perfect casing for the poo with the added environmental benefit of reusing and recycling. We set off, windows down and sunroof cracked open in a vain attempt to balance fresh air against the ongoing downpour, somehow making it to Dartmouth without expiring from the fumes. In normal circumstances we would have stopped to explore, but today, our mission was simply to locate a bin. It was very lucky for Doug that he waited until this point to suggest that the putrid smell might simply be the result of bad wrapping, as had the bin not been directly within sight, I might have been tempted to prove how DAMN WELL WRAPPED it was by unwrapping it layer by stinky layer right under his nose.

Learning point: *A bag of poo in the hand is*

worth three in the ~~bush~~ bin.

High point:

Regrouping in a Kingsbridge café: Scones, clotted cream, a handful of complimentary dog treats and no one batting an eyelid at us having Radar join us at the table. Well, under it to be precise but nothing would have surprised me here. This town is so dog-friendly that when I enquired at the information centre for any cafés that would accept dogs, the assistant gave me a perplexed look and announced that she could only think of one that wouldn't. For an instant, I was tempted to beg her for its location and sneak out the back door to abscond dog-free for an hour or so, but Radar was having none of it. Through the window his hopeful wagging tail and melty brown eyes bore through the glass and melted my heart. Again.

Friday 20th August

A day trip to the hippy vibes of Totnes. Lead forcibly by Radar towards a tasty display of doggy ice cream and a range of very funky dog collars we were sufficiently distracted to overlook my daughter's decision to dive into a hair salon and get her hair dyed red. I am sure the dog and her were in cahoots over this.

Saturday 21st August

Home again and it feels a bit like having completed your first marathon.

Not that I've ever actually run a marathon, nor do I have any intention of ever doing so, but, if I had I'm sure this is what it might feel like. A sense of achievement at having made it through, mixed with a level of exhaustion that puts into question whether you'd ever be mad enough to do it again.

The reality is, that on a dog holiday, everything has to be planned around the needs of the dog just like when you have a baby or small child. Poo bags, treats, leads and portable water bowls need to be carried. Routes and stopping places planned to cater for his toileting needs. Research carried out to check that your destination is dog friendly, and a blind hope that your canine friend will behave well enough not to upset anyone. It was fun, and a very different way to enjoy a holiday, but not exactly relaxing.

Monday 29th August

My husband and I are daringly going away together overnight. Don't get the wrong idea about this - the trip is not in itself particularly risky or thrill seeking. The danger is that we have left the dog and the kids in the care of my mother and her 80-year-old boyfriend for 24 hours. Mum is convinced that this will not be a problem and is no doubt envisaging a day of making cups of tea and cake to sit with in the garden whilst throwing the odd ball if the dog looks lively. I, however, am feeling physically sick at the thought of all the possible disastrous outcomes. Any concerns I've aired have been batted away as if I'm just an over-protective dog-mother with far less experience than them in these matters. I don't think they have any idea what a lively and mischievous handful he can be and have had to give Sascha strict instructions to take the lead (literally) on all excursions. I'm not sure whether I should be concerned more for the dog, the elderly parents or the kids who are probably the most competent of the bunch and will most likely end up looking after all involved. I am, however, also painfully aware that we haven't had time alone together as a couple for months and it is well overdue. Promising not to think about all this anymore, we head off to the bright lights of London and discover that, much like when Radar goes to the dog sitter's, it is entirely possible to run off with barely a backwards glance as the door closes behind us.

Tuesday 30th August

Twenty-four hours might not have been quite enough for us, but it was seemingly more than enough for those left at home. By breakfast time today, the texts were pinging in thick and fast.

Firstly, my mother.

"Hello darlings! Hope you're having a super time together. All is well here, and the dog is adapting very well to his new regime."

New regime? I was barely able to suppress an inner whimper of concern.

What was this 'new regime'?

What could possibly had occurred overnight to require it?

What level of bribery will Radar require to revert to his original routine THAT WE HAVE SPENT MONTHS WORKING ON?

I reassure myself that I'm probably reading too much into this very short and sweet text and sit back to focus on how many pains au chocolat I should take from the breakfast buffet to have with my coffee. A coffee that is currently being poured by a very handsome Italian waiter. He has an equally appealing accent that makes me want to ask him to repeat his question about whether there is anything else I need.

Unfortunately, this pleasant interlude is disturbed somewhat brutally by another shrill ping on my phone.

This time it is Sascha.

'Mum, please come home soon. My back is in

agony and I can't move. Have a list two pages long of things that have gone wrong.'

I am about to text back and explain that reception is very dodgy in this area and the transport links are quite unpredictable before remembering that not only would the very act of replying, blow such cover, but also that I am in central London, not some fogged out remote island in the Outer Hebrides.

Now there's an idea...

OK. Must stop. I am a responsible parent. Should not be fantasizing about the Outer Hebrides or breakfasts in Italy when my offspring are in need.

We return home to unravel what has been going on.

Radar is delighted to see us but, beyond a few enthusiastic wags, remains as tight lipped as ever and runs to find his chew toy.

My mother and her partner look well and relatively intact. In fact, dare I say quite smug to have proved themselves capable of holding the fort with a lively dog and two teenagers. They don't however hang around to share the details.

The kids look relieved and yet there is something simmering just under the surface. I guess babysitting two grandparents and a crazy dog can present some challenges.

Deep breath. Time to let them rant.

"Mum, that was awful. They have completely lost the plot and the dog is really traumatised."

Radar, unlike Sascha, looks decidedly chilled and unperturbed but I bite my tongue and nod soothingly as she lets rip with her double-sided disaster list. Momentarily my mind drifts to a calmer scene involving an Italian waiter serving me breakfast...

And then, Sascha's voice rises to a crescendo which crashes through this reverie too, announcing that the most embarrassing part of the last few hours was 'HIS RIDICULOUSLY HIGH SEX DRIVE'.

OK, I know I should have been 100% focussed on the conversation in hand, but they now had my full attention. I was also desperately trying to work out who she was referring to.

The Italian waiter? Please tell me I hadn't been thinking out loud?

Was it my 12-year-old son? Please no, not yet!

Or my mother's 80-year-old boyfriend? At that age...surely not?!

Or maybe, just maybe...the dog?

Ears now fully pricked, I listened with relief and rapture to Sascha describe the horror of Radar spending many of his waking hours rolling his favourite blanket up into a soft ball and then energetically humping it in the middle of the lounge every time the grandparents sat down to relax.

Radar remained unruffled by all this talk of his exploits, lying peacefully a few steps away from his blanket which had been abandoned carelessly in the middle of the floor for me to tidy up later. All thoughts of Italian breakfasts were now well and off the menu.

Friday 2nd September

6.15pm

The party is well and truly over. Maybe it's down to end of holiday blues and the looming return to school, but after a gruelling day topped off with a tsunami of demands and complaints from every direction, I decide that enough is enough and announce that I am LEAVING HOME. WITH THE DOG.

The second half of that declaration might seem misguided but bear with me - the dog might have his faults but he never comes into the kitchen moaning and stropping when dinner isn't ready for another forty minutes.

Not that the moaner (who will remain anonymous) had helped to prepare it, or not been offered a snack to stave off hunger pangs. No. But just because apparently, it's ok to mouth off to the one who plans, prepares and serves the dinner even if you are someone who switches between 'not being able to wait another second' for food, to 'not being that hungry anymore'. Grrrrr.

So, I announced my departure and absconded with the dog.

Somehow, I must have sounded scarily genuine as Doug looked openly shocked as I slammed the door behind me and left.

Because, you know what? Walking up a hill in the drizzle, even though I had just had my hair done hours earlier for my mum's 70th birthday lunch tomorrow, and then poo-picking (four times – each one sloppier than the last) made me feel so much better.

So, after 20 minutes of tramping my fury and indignation under mud splattered boots, Radar and I retraced our steps and went home.

And somehow, they hadn't killed each other or died of starvation. Doug had put the veg on and everyone sat down to eat without complaint.

Perhaps the advice of my colleague to have that suitcase always ready and packed in the event of needing to urgently abscond is quite a good one after all.

Saturday 3rd September

The kids have had a revelation. According to them, the reason, why the dog seems to so enjoy spending time at the dog sitter's and looks completely morose on his return to us is nothing to do with him enjoying the doggy equivalent of a play date, or even, if the latest reports are to be believed, a hot date that you don't want to end. It is rather that he is lonely and needs a friend. My eldest refused to budge on this opinion even when I pointed out that it was exactly this line of thinking that led us as parents to indulge her with a sibling – a decision that she has frequently questioned when Charlie exhibits the full extent of his ability to be the caricature of an annoying younger brother.

Charlie however is ignoring this line of argument to focus on the practical solutions to the problem and has declared that rather than spending all his savings on a ridiculously expensive upgrade to his mobile phone, he could invest instead in a pug. The first part of his argument, admittedly has legs... well, obviously so does the second but that is not the point. Such a thoughtful act of philanthropy to the dog's welfare can only be the result of the marvellous influence of generation YouTube whose kind-spirited focus on pug welfare has provided them with sanctuary in bedrooms from LA to London for generations to come.

So heart-warming.

Though not heart-warming enough to melt mine.

We are NOT getting another dog. Especially not a

pug.

How would you even walk a pug and a Labrador together? One would be jumping in the river, whilst the other would be pulling me home to get back to his livestream. It could never work.

EVER.

Wednesday 7th September

One minute we are happily walking up the hill enjoying a relaxed evening stroll; the next minute, Radar spots a jogger, who is seemingly so terrifying to him, that he turns on his tail and makes a run for home. He is clearly only focussed on saving his own neck, making no attempt to faithfully protect me from whatever terrible fate he has imagined is about to befall him. This bizarre and inexplicable panic is not helped by the fact that I had thrown caution to the wind and headed out in flipflops hoping to fully embrace this late summer warmth before it disappears. Clumsily, I somehow manage to catch the dog and regain control just as the jogger catches us up and attempts to prove to him that he is indeed worthy of befriending. This all seems rather odd. I'm impressed that this guy is making the effort but it's not as though Radar was going to attack them - he just wanted out. Personally, I don't blame him. Jogging up hills is no fun - downhill and home for biscuits is far more our style.

Anyway, it seems polite to show willing and so I try to reassure Radar that greeting this friendly looking jogger is a good idea. Within moments, the guy has sunk to his knees in front of the dog and is letting him lick his head. This seems a little extreme. Pretty sure this wasn't covered in the dog training classes. Perhaps he is some sort of dog whisperer? Radar is totally seduced by this and proceeds to roll on his back with his legs in the air having decided he wasn't so terrifying after all.

I am momentarily relieved until he mentions that following their recent relocation from the USA, they are looking forward to having their own dogs back with them soon. One of which is a large Alsatian type of dog, and the other is a chihuahua.

I think Radar must have instinctively sensed this before making friends with them. No one in their right minds would want to risk crossing a chihuahua.

Thursday 8th September

One moment, Radar and I were happily walking side by side up the hill, the next, he had darted through a hedge and completely disappeared. Two minutes of frantic calling elicited no response other than my own rising panic. What to do? Ring for back up? Would anyone get here before the trail went cold?

There was nothing for it but classic bribery and so, as I desperately alternated between shouting 'BISCUIT' and 'TREAT' at the top of my voice, it was with much relief that my Labrador came bursting through the undergrowth and heading straight for me.

Well, it was a sort of relief.

In the time it had taken him to get lost in the hedge and find his way back to me, Radar had somehow managed to change the colour of his colour of his collar from red to blue. I stood momentarily questioning how this could have come to pass, when a cyclist appears over the hill to reclaim blue-collared lab for himself, with Radar, red collar still intact, trotting happily alongside his bike.

Do you think that anyone has ever gone out for a walk and come home with the wrong dog? I mean, as much as I would like to say that I would recognise my dog anywhere, all that lineage and breeding can go a long way towards creating some very indistinguishable dogs. Imagine if the cyclist had a preference for red?

Friday 9th September

The dog has been discovered in the garden with the remains of a well-licked tub of olive oil spread. Licked by him that is, not us. We hadn't even had a look in. Blame for who had left such a treasure out for Radar to enjoy, ricochets back and forth across the house; but the bottom line is that in the next few hours we are probably looking at some sort of very messy explosion from at least one end of the dog.

We line the floor with newspaper, and I then very swiftly head out to book club in the hope that the moment may pass in my absence.

…

11pm: Still no ill effects. This is not entirely comforting. It will be a nail-biting night.

Saturday 10th September

By some miracle, there has been no explosion. However, as the first up (why me? How do they all get away with it?), and despite the heavy rain, I'm taking no chances. We exit the house before breakfast and head without delay to the nearest open space, armed with plenty of poo bags. I stand and wait, in what is now a torrential downpour, for Radar to empty his bowels, reassuring myself that in this weather, any residual mess will be quickly washed away. Nothing happens. Not jack sh**.

 Learning point: *A watched pup never poops.*

Thursday 15th September

The problem with trying to be a responsible dog owner and pick up your dog's poo, is that on every walk there is plenty of evidence that a lot of other owners just aren't bothering. Nonetheless, fearing a fine, or even a future bit of negative karma by treading in my own dog's mess, I duly bag it up. Today however, the stench is too much to bear, so I decide to leave the bag on a branch, ready to collect as we walk past at the end of our walk. This would have been the perfect plan if I hadn't then completely forgotten about the abandoned bag until we got home, forcing me to suffer the inconvenience and awkwardness of going back to get it and then finding myself walking through the village with a bag of poo in one hand and no dog in the other.

Moral of the day: *A bag in the bush is worth... oh you can complete the rest.*

The poo bag is finally consigned to the dustbin and I indulge in a sigh of relief at having finally made it back home. This is almost immediately broken by Charlie, who looks unusually overwrought and upset, announcing that he is beginning to feel that getting a dog is the biggest mistake we ever made.

Right.

I am slightly confused by this. He has had to do

little more than give the dog a friendly passing stroke today, and though I'm tempted to point this out and launch into a comment about having to retrace steps to collect bags of poo, I bite my tongue and ask him to tell me more.

He tells me that he is feeling sad that he doesn't feel what he had hoped to for Radar, and that he was really missing his cat who died a year or so back. He felt as though Radar had taken his place causing the cat to be forgotten.

This caught me by surprise and quite off-guard, but it does open the door to a conversation about the inevitability of change, death and how our feelings for pets, as well as people in our lives, can alter and develop over time. Whilst I don't want Charlie to feel sad about the situation, perhaps this is part of what having a pet is all about – they can be a valuable steppingstone in learning about some of the more challenging aspects of life and death, love and responsibility.

I found myself choosing to point out the huge benefits of having a dog in the family - and whilst there might have a been a small voice in the back of my mind asking if I really believed my own words, I think fundamentally that I did. It is difficult at times, but Radar is becoming as much a part of the family as everyone else and the challenges of family life are, I think, a constant for all of us, as much as the pleasures. Perhaps dogs really are good for our souls.

Friday 16th September

I return home to discover that most of the downstairs and much of the garden is littered with shredded wood. For a bit of variety, the lounge floor was also covered in a shredded crisp packet and a pizza box following a theft from the recycling bin. No one had seemingly had a moment to remedy the situation and so I spent the evening raging alone against the mess.

The garden had to be swept with Radar shut in the house as he still can't resist leaping on the broom and seizing it between his jaws every time it moves. I even considered hoovering the garden, which might seem extreme but would have been a far quicker way of collecting the shreds of wood. In fact, apart from the odd looks that I might have got from any neighbours flicking the net curtains, it would have been the perfect solution. Or at least it would have been the perfect solution if I hadn't then discovered that the hoover had been taken to the garage and attached to some sort of large contraption. With Doug out at a physio appointment, and reaching the back of the garage to decode the purpose of said contraption and how to dismantle it feeling like a stretch too far, I stuck with the broom. Simultaneously repeating the mantra from yesterday's philosophical musings that having a dog is good for our souls. I might have to repeat this a few more times.

Saturday 17th September

Warning: Clear and pheasant danger!

Sorry. Couldn't resist that.

But don't get me wrong - this is a serious point. It turns out that we have reached the time of year when a pheasant release is imminent. This means that in the very same rural areas where highly trained working dogs such as Spaniels and Labradors abound, flocks of young, naive pheasants will be released into every hedgerow you pass. This in turn leads to a game of stealth and subterfuge between pheasant, dog, dog owner and the truly terrifying figure of The Game Keeper.

For the next four months, The Game Keeper will stalk these hills, seeking out innocent dog owners who dare to let their pets off the lead and risk the lives of his young birds. If you succumb to such degenerate behaviour, be warned, that justifying it as fair game (on a roll today!) in the light of the fact that he has carelessly released such tempting fare into the wild ready to be killed later in the season anyway, will get you nowhere. When this first happened to me, I was raging so furiously from the request to walk my dog on a lead until February, that I proceeded to investigate the issue from every legal standpoint I could imagine, before deciding that there are bigger battles to fight and reverting to my more natural live and let live philosophy.

And then planning an underground counterattack.

Well, not literally underground. That would be pointless, most unpleasant and spoil the view.

No, I was going to win by stealth.

I worked out that there were three sections to my walk – The Initial Hill, The Long Stretch and The Forest.

The Initial Hill was cleared for free running and so no lead was required, and The Forest was too far off the beaten track to be easily patrolled; but the key area for being accosted by The Game Keeper was at section two – The Long Stretch.

This was where my plan had to unfold.

Fortunately, on this stretch, there is excellent visibility in all directions and with it being open and flat, there is also a good chance that you will hear the rumblings of The Game Keeper's Land Rover before it comes into sight. So, with ears pricked and eyes peeled, I can release Radar to run, and then quickly retrieve him with a tasty treat if I hear the slightest hint of engine noise. The beauty of this, is that I can trick TGK into seeing me as an impeccably responsible and considerate dog owner, whilst managing to give the dog the freedom to run.

This is a marvellously cunning plan!

Or at least I was brimming with cunning confidence until, right on cue, the ominous purr of an engine forced me to swiftly stop daydreaming and put the plan into action.

Gulp.

Grabbing the lead and hoping not to draw attention to our rule-breaking by loudly calling him to heel, I uttered a series of desperate whispered hisses.

'Radar - come!'

'COME'

'COME! FFS...BISCUITS!'

Nothing.

Ignoring me completely, salvation came only by Radar's determination to continue chewing at a large clump of juicy grass. With a leap, I looped the noose around his neck like a clumsy cowgirl, regaining composure within the nick of time, just as the Land Rover drew to a halt to pause perfectly at our heels.

Somehow, I managed to utter a cheery 'Good morning!' whilst inwardly planning an innocent explanation as to why the dog might have been momentarily roaming free within sniffing distance his precious pheasants.

THE GAME KEEPER's response was not what I expected. Leaning his craggy and weather-beaten head out of the window, he thanked me for my responsible approach and how refreshing it was that I understood his position. Naturally, I smiled agreeably and wished him luck with the season, with just a tiny twinge of guilt at this blinding success.

Admittedly, Radar has yet to develop a hunting instinct, as I think that even these magnificent levels of stealth might be thwarted by having to wrangle a wriggling pheasant from his chops in exchange for a treat before we were caught red-~~handed~~-mouthed.

Tuesday 20th September

Rumour has it that there have been a couple of burglaries in the village this week and so the community is on high alert and I am feeling relieved to be the owner of a large man-eating dog.

Well, I say 'man-eating', but that's just to scare away any opportunist intruders. Unfortunately, he is showing signs of wanting to welcome them in a far too friendly manner and even entice them into his domain with the offer of overly-flirtatious licks and soggy tennis balls.

He has however shown, on at least one occasion, that he can act in a manner that would make Doggywood proud and win him that Oscar, by looking uncharacteristically fierce as we walked past two rather suspicious-looking men, lurking without purpose, as we headed out on a walk.

He refused to offer them a wag and obediently marched past with an unpredictable look in his eye, as I gruffly instructed 'LEAVE' as we passed, giving the impression that they had been narrowly spared an aggressive attack by a barely controllable Labrador. With his normal response being to roll on his back and stick his legs in the air or run in the opposite direction in the face of danger, it was truly a winning performance. Brave Radar, the prima donna guard dog!

Wednesday 21st September

Definitely a bad dog day.

So bad it needs bulleting.

- Dog goes nuts on his short evening walk, returning to the days of randomly leaping up at me and grabbing my arm with his mouth. I don't understand why he does this and it's really getting me down, scaring me and worrying me.
- The moment I make it home, I can smell nothing but dog poo. I can only assume that it's smeared onto my clothes as a result of being wildly leapt at, so rip them all off and head straight for a shower.
- I am feeling like a helicopter parent. Whilst my heart wants him to be able to run free and learn to socialise calmly, I am so worried about him leaping

overexcitedly at a young child or elderly person, that I feel that I can't let him off the lead, which results in an even more lively and frustrated dog than before. I have no idea what to do about this apart from finding walks that are so off the beaten track that only the toughest of intrepid toddlers and elderly explorers are likely to cross our path.

- Another evening of multitasking a dog walk in the last of the evening light with cooking a dinner that will be criticised by at least one of the recipients who are currently very busy on their computers: One is fighting dragons; another is flying a plane and the third is battling some GCSE maths questions. Only the latter is forgiven, although she may just be a little more strategic in her choice of excuse.

- Hormones: I am either premenstrual, peri-menopausal or just pi**ed off.... but either way, I feel like a raging fireball of frustration with the fakest of crocodilian smiles and soon will add the tears to match.

Thursday 22nd September

Learning point: *The degree of trainability afforded by your dog's obsession with food is directly proportional to amount of slobber produced when you are eating your favourite dinner.*

Do not be fooled. A Labrador's insatiable appetite is not simply a useful attribute with which to blackmail him through his training needs. What you will not be told in the doggy guidebooks is that this very trait will also multiply ten-fold the effort you have to put in to have a pleasant family meal.

Two options might present themselves:

1. You may choose to distance yourself from your dog while eating. Obvious you might think, but, turning those 'starving' melty brown eyes away from the dining table and potentially hearing the disappointed whimpers from a distance is enough to melt many a heart. In this respect, Labradors are much like those infamous hungry gremlins. Be warned.

Or,

2. Allow your dog to be near you while eating and take advantage of what could be a perfect example of the genius of biology and evolution working in

perfect synchronicity. As the dog drools endlessly, he is compelled to behave impeccably and perfect his adoring gaze, whilst you are increasingly discouraged from enjoying the delicacies on your plate due to the Niagara Falls of slobber falling from his chops. This results in you passing increasing quantities of leftovers to your loving, obedient pup. Your fellow diners may well find the situation so repulsive that they abandon the table to eat elsewhere or are put off their dinner entirely. I guess this might be the go-to option for those on a diet or those who find the table manners of their fellow diners intolerable.

I'd like to soften this reality with the suggestion that a dog's appreciation of your culinary offerings is a compliment to the irresistible flavours and gourmet quality of your cuisine.

That however would be a lie.

The reason dogs are just as happy to indulge in licking a pile of cow dung as a sirloin steak is that their sense of taste is completely different to ours and far less potent, having only around 1700 taste buds to our 9000! If, however, you are a producer of high-end mineral water bottled from pure mountain streams nurtured by water nymphs, you might like to consider a new market for your product: Apparently dogs can taste water...who knew that was even possible?!

Friday 23rd September

Just to further sweeten any residual taste bud trauma from yesterday's revelations, I must share with you that Radar has developed a taste for foraging. He will happily walk to heel with the offer of a juicy blackberry just as with a meaty treat. I can't tell you how marvellous it is to think that for a few weeks a year I can venture out without a pocket full of meaty treats that make me eminently muggable and my tissues smell of concentrated game. He also likes foraging cow dung but we are not going to discuss this.

Saturday 24th September

I had almost forgotten that Radar has a slight issue with runners until this afternoon.

At least, he did have an issue with runners.

Today's events prove that my remedial training on this matter has resolved this issue so effectively, that instead of running a mile from them, he now likes to join them on their journey. Thanks to his previous encounter he now assumes that all runners want to be his friend and will ultimately bow down before him and let him lick their heads.

So, there we were, just reaching the brow of the hill, enjoying a moment of carefree daydreaming, when, caught off guard by my reverie, a runner appeared from around the bend, to be greeted by a bouncing and overexcited Radar. Being still on the uphill trajectory and a few paces behind, I was forced to break into a run myself to try to grab him from the runner's path, but by this point Radar had turned it into a great game, bouncing down the hill alongside the runner, nimbly avoiding my desperate grasps and deaf to any instructions.

"I'm really sorry – he has a thing for runners" I gasp breathlessly, with an attempt at a conciliatory smile.

The response is a gruff grunt of disapproval and a seriously pi**ed-off glare.

I am suddenly struck by the idea that Radar might have had a point when he previously ran from a similar scenario and decide this is my best course of action. Not in fear of course – that would have set a terrible example to my newly runner-recovered dog. No, this was to be purely strategic: By breaking into a run, not only would I surely become more tempting bait for my dog to chase, but he might also panic at my impending absence and return immediately to my heels.

By some miracle, this works. But not without the echo of an expletive from said runner as I run for the hills. Going back to explain my strategy didn't seem like an option.

With any luck that would be the first and last time we crossed paths.

To finish me off, Radar, still utterly hyped, gets another case of the the Zoomies* doing a grand job of leaping and jumping at me and his lead as we head for home. This is not fun.

*This is a newly appropriated phrase, faking itself as an official definition, which will here on in be used to describe his moments of aggressive leaping madness.

Sunday 25th September

Doug has offered to walk the dog with me this-evening. I interpret this as moral support after yesterday's events, which I'm sure is what he intended. Unfortunately, our interpretations of moral support are somewhat different. I'd have liked him to manage the dog and just join me on the walk, chatting perhaps about non-dog things, but the reality is that his version of moral support is to turn the walk into a second-by-second dog training session. This involves him giving me constant loud and clear instructions that I need to get word perfect and with the right intonation at the precise moment they are required. This has the effect of making me hugely self-conscious about everything I'm doing and even less effective. Perhaps if I'd been in a better frame of mind, I *might* have appreciated this, but instead I feel like punching him or curling up in ball and crying at the challenges of bringing up our 'third child'.

Maybe tomorrow I'll be able to face this head on and embrace becoming some sort of dog super-parent...but for now, I'm going to bury my head in the sand.

Monday 26th September

I have left to walk the dog alone because I secretly can't bear to be subjected to another training session. I know I should be broader shouldered than this, but these ideological differences are beginning to come between us. Stomping up the hill, inwardly still raging and rather miserable, I am stopped in my tracks by a friendly cocker spaniel and his owner.

The dogs decide that we are heading in the same direction and we quickly slip into a gentle exchange of training stories as she describes how her husband has a completely different training style to her. He will greet the dog with joyous enthusiasm rather than her more tempered gentle stroke. Long drawn out instructions will be relayed to the dog on when he can fetch his food, 'Just wait a moment...', 'No..not yet, you need to be a good boy', rather than her simple 'sit!', 'Fetch' and an clear hand signal. If I'm honest, put like that, I can see her point, but although I don't admit it, I can see myself leaning more towards her husband's style...perhaps I'm reverting to trying to cajole a recalcitrant toddler rather than a dog?

Tuesday 27th September

Ok. I've shaken off the sand, rubbed it out of my eyes and decided that with a day off today, I'll brave a walk through the village trialling Doug's latest dog training suggestions.

And would you believe it?! Bingo!

Within moments the dog has tried to leap up and mug me for treats. Immediately I put into action stage two, which is to place my foot on the lead at exactly the right length to prevent him from leaping off the ground. This simple move completely takes the wind out of his sails and in his confusion at my inexplicably invincible control, Radar stops and asks slightly more politely for the treat. He even manages to succumb to such bribery when encouraged to pass an ageing golden retriever without leaping at her. The owner, clearly seeing through his 'obedience' to the core of my plight through eyes of time worn experience, reassures me that in years to come I will look back fondly on the days when my young energetic hound pulls my arm out of its sockets with his enthusiasm for life.

I know she is right. But I also know I'm in for a long wait.

To hammer in this point, the day hasn't finished with us yet.

Two hours later:

The first thing that struck me was that Radar wasn't wagging enthusiastically at the door when I returned from the school run. He wouldn't even raise himself from his bed with anything more than an almost indiscernible wag of the tail. What's more, his face looks disturbingly mis-shaped and on closer inspection it appears that his cheek has swollen up to the size of a golf ball. Within moments I am on the phone to the vet hoping that this is one of the three afternoons when they have a surgery running from the local farm and that there isn't a long queue of incapacitated cows or sheep ahead of us.

Thanks goodness, our luck was in and Radar was offered a slot for an hour and a half later.

I spend this hour and a half anxiously alternating between pacing the room and trying to work out if the swelling is growing bigger. What if it was an allergic reaction? Was his throat about to swell up and send him into anaphylactic shock? Can we last an hour and a half? After thirty minutes, torn between neuroticism and responsibility, I rang the vet again to check we were still ok to wait.

As ever, the vet proves to be an immediate

soothing balm. He reckons that it is probably just a wasp sting and a suggests administering a bag of frozen peas until we can get him up to the surgery.

Why didn't I think of that?

I am now sheepishly feeling like an overprotective and slightly neurotic mother. Again.

One steroid injection and £66 later, the 'wasp sting' is under control and Radar seems fine. I make a mental note to ensure I always have a plentiful supply of frozen peas available in the event of this ever happening again.

Panic over.

Friday 30th September

Learning point – *notes on the etiquette of poo – Autumn edition:*

It turns out that there really is a complex etiquette as to where one should abandon a bag of poo. Ideally of course the nearest bin would be the perfect solution to avoiding a long walk carrying a package of Eau-de-Excrement, but in rural areas this may simply not be an option. And of course, all abandoning should be a temporary fix with the ultimate intention of retrieving the bag on your return journey.

So where to leave it? The ground is a definite no-no. Such carefree abandon would soon lead to it being trodden and ripped resulting in a plastic-polluted mess of the very type you sought to avoid in the first place.

Hanging it from a bush seems to be a more popular option. If hung at eye level, what you lose in aesthetics is gained in the chance that you might remember to collect on your return. Note however, that at this time of the year, you should not under any circumstances attach your poo bag in the vicinity of a blackberry bush. Not only is the potential for spikes piercing your bag exponentially increased, but you run the risk of being spotted by a local forager and incurring a wrath for which THE GAME KEEPER was only the training ground.

Monday 10th October

Moral of the day: *A head torch is not just for caving, It's for poo picking.*

With the nights drawing in it is becoming clear that a new accessory for night-time excursions with the dog is required: A head torch.

Somewhat naïve to the demands of moonlit dog walking, I had thought that dressing up like a caver was a little extreme for a short evening toilet trip but having failed abysmally at the alternative of attempting to hold a lead, a torch and pick up a poo simultaneously, getting over any issues with sporting the caver/mountaineer/ night-fishing look is proving to be an important part of dog ownership.

So, tonight was the night for test-driving my new head torch and I am now in the position to offer to some valuable words of wisdom from this experience:

- Do not attempt to begin opening newly purchased torches packaged in super-strong plastic that requires wire cutters to open, after you have announced to your dog that it is time for a walk and put on your coat. His excitement will not ease the process.
- Ensure scissors/wire cutters/axe or similar are easily available long in advance of the walk.
- Build in time for deciphering the opening mechanism for the battery compartment.
- Build in time for working out how to turn it on after you have completed the above steps.
- Having finally succeeded with all the above, bear in mind that the elasticated head attachment requires serious adjustment if it not to fall over your eyes or pop off.
- This prior point becomes particularly relevant if your dog chooses to alternate

his pace. This may lead your carefully positioned torch to dislodge, resulting in a very fetching glowing snout or luminous gas mark look if you're into that kind of thing.

· If all this seems too much, take comfort in the fact that if you coordinate your head torch with a delinquent style hoody, you will not only be completely incognito, but will dazzle* anyone who crosses your path.

*To clarify, this is a literal, blinding type of dazzle, not the metaphorical version where fans fall on their knees in front of you, so stunned as they are by your brilliance. Although they might fall in front of you due to missing their step after you blinded them.

· Do not kid yourself that this is the end of the matter. By the end of a few walks under such conditions, you will realise that whilst you are by no means alone in wandering the streets at night with a headtorch, you and your dog may feel peer pressure to add a luminous jacket and perhaps a flashing collar to your outfits.

Saturday 29th October

I am becoming increasingly concerned that one of my most dog-resistant friends is being slowly and unwittingly seduced by The Lure of The Dog. In fact, it is the very insidious nature of this contagious and often incurable condition that is one of the cornerstones of my commitment to writing this book. Too many have fallen before her, and with the kinship of friendship in mind, offering a guiding hand through this rite of passage, feels like the right thing to do.

Surely then, you can imagine my concern when, whilst out running together, she casually mentions what a lovely riverside walk she had with her friend's dog and how she could see the real benefits of owning and exploring with a canine pal.

Now, many of us might simply respond with an agreeable nod at this stage, but such comments should not be taken lightly. Especially if your friend has disliked the idea of a dog for decades, has a husband who is seriously allergic to them and until this point has avoided pets of any kind. It is at times like this that you really need to be a true and brutally honest friend.

Whether due to the pace of the run or concern over the direction her affliction was heading, I could do little but inwardly gasp and maintain a non-committal silence. Perhaps stopping her in her tracks and checking her vital signs would have been the right move, but this might have messed with her Strava record and I needed to keep her on side in this moment of madness.

Cold hard logic and reasoned argument was probably the best strategy and as luck would have it, I had an ace up my sleeve.

It just so happened that a couple of days ago, my neighbours had recommended the very same riverside walk, around the back of the beautiful city of Winchester. It should be mentioned at this point that they do not have a dog. They were however, particularly taken with the route, due to its artistic potential and opportunities to stop and take in the tranquillity of the riverside setting. Admittedly, such thoughts appealed greatly to my romantic side and so, I barely gave a second thought, when faced with the mixed blessing of an enforced wait in Kwik Fit to fix a nail puncture in my tyre, to filling that time by taking Radar for a stroll along that exact stretch of the river.

There are two things that I have to say about this:

1. It was not a stroll.
2. My delight at being coincidentally and practically shod in a new pair of long-awaited Timberland boots as my tyre was being fixed, was short-lived.

The route itself was idyllic, having chosen to take the scenic tow path adjacent to the river, running along the backs of a row of tucked away riverside cottages. Radar rapidly realised that this was a fabulous adventure and took the lead, dragging me unpredictably along the narrow path, desperately dodging brambles as he jolted me in the direction of every delicious unexamined smell. The alternative path would have been a couple of metres wide and gravelled. This one was not only less than one abreast, but it was muddy, slippery and perilously close to the water's edge. My newly unboxed boots might just have kept me upright, but by the time we reached the end of the path, they were also covered in mud.

Radar must have sensed my distress and adeptly resolved this issue, as well as his own of wearing a fur coat on a remarkably mild autumn afternoon, by making a sudden leap from the bank into the cooling depths of the water with me still attached firmly to the other end of his lead.

I will say no more of this. The resulting clean boots were little consolation. But I did recount this reality check to my friend and have heard no more from her since about the delights of walking dogs by rivers. Mission accomplished.

Thursday 3rd November

Learning point: *Labradors have impeccable fashion sense. Your dog may not verbalise that your outfit makes you look ever so slightly ridiculous and verging on the insane, but if he rolls on the ground and clamps his legs together to avoid dressing in the same way, follow his example.*

It is a pitch-black night. Tipping it down with rain and I have mislaid the head torch. There is an urgency to Radar's need for a walk and so no time to hunt down the missing torch. There is nothing for it but to head out unequipped.

The dog chose these conditions and my foolhardy decision to rely on a mobile phone for light, to deposit the entire contents of his bowels on the lawn in front of the Baptist church. Not just in one easily retrievable pile, but in multiple positions. Clearly there is something wrong with his stomach - no sooner had he deposited in one spot, then it was time to leap to the next. With my hands full of leads and my light shining in all the wrong places, opening a plastic poo bag was proving a challenge too far. Locating the deposits in what was rapidly becoming a minefield of sh** whilst stooping, drenched and bedraggled in headlights of every passing car, might seem the epitome of responsible dog ownership, but the reality is just embarrassing.

I think that perhaps the dog did this on purpose.

You see, what I failed to mention earlier, was that we were both dressed in newly purchased luminous jackets.

To be fair, Radar had tried to save us from the humiliation of such costumes by chewing his jacket and running round in circles as I tried to put it on him. The jackets were now making me feel like a cheaply dressed Halloween trick or treater who'd stayed out a few days too long and I was paying the consequences for my stubborn perseverance.

Radar was also sporting a brightly flashing collar, with an enviable range of three different flash settings. No, I take that back – I must have momentarily got carried away on the marketing. In no way do I feel tempted to invest in a triple-flashing dog collar to add to my outfit or to ask Radar to lend me his.

Friday 4th November

Learning point: *If the above account in any way discourages you from investing in a range of luminous accessories, fear not. I can offer two top tips for the price of one: Dressing your dog is much easier if you allow them to chew on a delicious meat filled dog bone as you attach their coat. Even if this does result in your carpets smelling of rotting meat, or the bone being accidentally dropped on your toes. The latter at least, is easily resolved by getting yourself a pair of steel toed boots to wear with your luminous jacket.*

I felt this was a far more positive set of pointers to share today rather than the moment that involved us being lynched by an untethered growling Alsatian at the very moment when I was trying to keep a one-handed hold on Radar in order to seal a perilously full poo bag in the other.

Saturday 5th November

One of the things I love about having a dog are the endless opportunities to head out for a walk with friends and let the dogs run and play freely, and this-afternoon Radar got to meet up with one of his favourites – the blonde Alsatian who added highlights to my black trousers at last year's New Year's Eve party (I'm still not over this, but am too good a friend with her owner to let it come between us).

The downside of this is that is doesn't take much to get engrossed in conversation and just at the worst possible moment, let down your guard. This worse possible moment materialised as we reached the top of the hill, up to our elbows in an analysis of how we'd ended up with dogs just as our children were beginning to take flight, when we wandered onto The Long Stretch. That same long stretch that requires constant vigilance against the possibility of entrapment by TGK.

We however, had forgotten all about him, it now being so deep into the shooting season we had become somewhat blasé about the possibility of bumping into him. It was therefore quite a shock to find his Land Rover heading straight for us, with no time to even pretend that the dogs were on the lead. Trundling to a halt, blocking our path, he wound down his window with a delighted glint in his eye at having caught such easy prey on his rounds. A captive audience to his fury, we endured a tirade of declarations that our dogs were a threat to his pheasants and that we were right on the edge of a shoot area and must keep the dogs on the leads. Quite where these edges are, it was impossible to know and debating the concept that his birds were released free to roam – nay, even trespass into my garden on occasion, didn't seem strategically wise. Between gritted teeth we smiled innocently, nodding in appropriate places and secretly swearing to ignite a vicious legal battle for the freedom to roam, a pledge that lasted all of the 10 minutes it took for us to tire of googling 'could my dog be shot for chasing a pheasant' or 'is lead wearing enforceable on public footpaths'. Pretty sure there wasn't a pheasant within miles of us by the time our dogs had made their presence known.

Monday 7th November

Radar's sexuality is developing at quite a pace. Not in the least bit fussy about gender, today he became very excited by being mounted by a blonde, fluffy and gently lolloping labradoodle, described by his owner as 'more of a lover than a fighter'. Marvellous! What a way to live!

Wednesday 9th November

OMG – did you know that you can buy dog jumpers that disguise your pooch as a reindeer in every size imaginable?

Sorry, but I am just a little over-excited.

What started off as a simple trip to the pet store to stock up on poo bags and training treats, became an eye-opening (and eye-wateringly extravagant) Christmas shopping expedition. I had no idea of the levels to which you could indulge your dog at this time of year.

Actually, let's be honest, this isn't entirely about indulging the dog - I'm not sure Radar would have looked at the reindeer outfits in quite the same light as me as I imagined him leaping through the fields on Christmas day proudly bearing the smartest of antlers and being adored for his expression of seasonal jollity by everyone we pass.

His version might have been something closer to 'If you think that a Labrador of my breeding and pedigree is going to go out on Christmas day dressed even more humiliatingly than the pathetic attempt you made last week to dress me as a glowing Halloween ghoul on the grounds of health and safety, I will drag you and your only slightly more tasteful cashmere reindeer jumper out into the garden and s*** on it. Before accidentally flicking my overexcited tail in the vicinity of the newly-filled champagne glasses.'

(I don't actually own a cashmere reindeer jumper, but he knows I've been lusting after a particularly cute one having spotted me drooling over a website a couple of days ago. I take this as a gentle warning).

Perhaps the bowties or waistcoats in Harris Tweed would have been more his style?

After much debate, he will, among other things, wake up on Christmas morning to a two-metre length of squeaky plastic ivy, some seasonal meaty chews and a Santa hat. Just so he doesn't feel left out.

Moral of the day: *Christmas is absolutely for dogs, even if a dog should never be just for Christmas.*

(See what I did there? Be warned; this is what happens when you are overcome by the aroma of red and green-themed seasonal meaty chews)

Saturday 12th November

Pheasants are rapidly becoming the bane of our lives. Well, not so much Radar's – he thinks that they are fair game (sorry, still getting over the meaty chew fumes) and he is now so attuned to their scent that his recall has dropped through the floor. The dog trainers have therefore recommended a month of walks on the extendable lead until he calms down. I am convinced that they are in cahoots with THE GAME KEEPER.

This is very bad news. Radar needs to run. A walk on the lead doesn't even get close to burning off all his energy and there is no way that I'm running with him. I tried it once and it didn't end well. Radar was so overexcited by the whole idea that he turned it into a dystopian game of chase, casting the two of us as predator and prey. No prizes for deducing which role he allocated to me.

And what if even after a month on the lead he doesn't improve? Will we be facing a lifetime of being dragged up hill and down dale? My knees and shoulders will be wrecked, and no doubt my hands ripped to shreds by the aforementioned laser-sharp edges of the extendable lead that I am still no further along in mastering.

What sort of life lesson could he possibly be training us for that will require us to restrict exercise and everyday freedom of movement? This dog really does exhibit some very peculiar behaviour.

Saturday 19th November

On a positive note, the stockpile of treats purchased alongside the doggy stocking fillers, have proved a real bonus in keeping Radar's mind off the pheasants as we trek dutifully tethered together. Despite my frustrations on this situation, we were rewarded for our vigilance by bumping into TGK again today who reverted to cheerily praising my responsible attitude. I have no idea if he recognised me from his tirade a few days ago, but my reluctant smile in return for his appreciation was harder to fake. This is not much fun and unlike the dog, a couple of treats and a pat on the back do little to sweeten things. Pretty sure this is further irrefutable evidence of the dog trainer/TGK conspiracy.

And then there was the back-handed compliment we got at dog training today, where the feistiness of Radar's personality was deemed so challenging, that the trainer said that if we hadn't persevered to such an extent, he is exactly the sort of dog that many would have put up for re-homing.

To be honest, whilst it clearly wasn't intended as such, this was a bit of a body blow. In fact, when I recounted this to my daughter, she was almost brought to tears. The thought of rehoming this, slightly nuts but now much-loved, member of the family was a really quite upsetting. Sure, there had been challenges, but nothing that hadn't come up whilst raising two children.

Had our challenges this year really been that much worse than other people's?

I don't think so...

And this is perhaps the point – raising a dog isn't

easy. Some days it's really rubbish. You might want to hand them back; you might want to blame it on the rest of the household for luring you into this, or, maybe, with an overflowing bucket-load of patience, you might end up with a companion who ultimately starts to feel like the only sane member of the pack.

I guess, now that I've picked my jaw up off the floor, that this is what the dog trainers were getting at - we'd started to see that light at the end of the tunnel.

Monday 21st November

Today, Radar managed to gate-crash his way onto a shoot. Stumbling across a party of tweeded gentry and their accompanying Labradors snootily focussed on retrieving pheasants conveniently raining down from above, it became abundantly clear that Radar was unable to buck the breeding of his bloodline. No sooner had he sniffed the air and caught a drifting waft of fowl, he was in his element.

Of course, his interest may have been piqued by the scent of freshly homemade sausage rolls drifting from the picnic baskets in the back of the Land Rovers, but either way, his patient admiration of the proceedings was rewarded with us both being given a sausage roll for the road.

As if to prove his dedication, and by some remarkable coincidence, we sat down this-evening to watch television and what should come up but a rural shoot scene! Whether it was the sound of the guns suggesting the imminent thrill of the chase, or the excited barks of the on-screen Labradors looking for sausage rolls to fall from the sky, I couldn't say, but he was hooked.

I am unsure what to do about this. The shooting season is now in full swing and no doubt if we take this route again, he will doggedly insist that we sit nicely and wait to be given a tasty treat until he becomes so entrenched in the scene that he gets invited to join this elite club. But this is not my idea of fun. Standing for hours in a muddy field, rain pouring down, a biting November chill creeping through my coat, hoping that my dog behaves in a civilised and controlled manner (Ha!), when instead, if the urge for roast pheasant ever became overpowering, a short trip to the butchers would probably suffice.

Perhaps we could find an alternative walking route for the season.

Tuesday 22nd November

There is a strange phenomenon occurring with the Christmas TV adverts this year. Every one of them seems to feature the delights of having a dog to partake in your festivities.

This is hugely reassuring as we have decided to break the mould this year and spend Christmas in Wales in a rented cottage by the sea. What's more, we are bringing my mother with us.

And the dog.

And planning to cook a Christmas Day dinner for everyone including my mother-in law, her partner and a couple of my husband's step-brothers.

To ensure this is utterly stress-free, Christmas lunch has been purchased from Cook, I've got a Sainsbury's delivery slot booked to the cottage and so it should be a simple matter of following the instructions minute by minute and producing a faultless feast single-handedly.

If the following adverts are anything to go by, having a supportive canine by my side will guarantee that this will be an unreserved success.

Sainsbury's decided that the disaster wreaked by the family cat in last year's advert (basically he burned the house down on Christmas Eve leaving the family nothing but a blackened turkey and a charcoaled shell of a home to wake up to on Christmas morning) warranted a change of tack.

This year their advert features the much safer option of the family dog, as his owner, an overwrought dad trying to make everything perfect for Christmas day, comes to realise, to the tune of a heart-rending chorus finale of 'woof woof' by the dog, that just being there is enough. I like this message – especially the concept that the husband organises the whole of Christmas. Not sure we've quite reached this level of gender equality though in our household and actually, even in the advert the guy gets so stressed trying to multitask, that he resorts to cloning both himself and the dog in order to get everything done on time. I am finding it uncannily easy to identify with his predicament, but feel that a Christmas with multiple husbands on the verge of a breakdown and a pack of bouncing Labradors could perhaps backfire?

John Lewis took a slightly different slant on this. Their advert features Buster the Boxer who looks on enviously as two foxes, a badger and a couple of squirrels get to play on the newly constructed trampoline in the garden, ready to be revealed on Christmas morning. Such is Buster's excitement as the doors open to the garden for the little girl to enjoy her gift, that he cannot hold back, overtakes her and leaps on, leaving her to watch incredulously from the side lines. I'm having flashbacks to birthday celebrations over the last few months where Radar's enthusiasm for tearing wrapping open and risking destruction of the contents might have to be carefully managed.

And then there is Marks and Spencer. This story features a dog named Tiger - a moniker that suggests they had learned nothing from their competitor's disaster movie last year. Sure enough, disaster strikes as the unfortunately named dog destroys the elder daughter's favourite shoes. But all is not lost – Christmas is saved by the kind request to Santa from the younger brother to replace the shoes. An enviably glamorous Mrs Claus manages to intercept this last-minute plea and seamlessly hand delivers them by helicopter (which of course she pilots herself) before returning to lounge on the sofa reading Fifty Shades of Red just as Santa comes in from the cold. I am confident that this tale of powerful feminine prowess, sensual glamour, sibling love and ultimately, a well-behaved dog, will define our Christmas exactly.

Wednesday 23rd November

Radar has returned from the dog sitter's today with a beaming smile on his face.

No really - it turns out that dogs can actually smile! Radar learnt this bit of canine charm from his mother, though you'd be forgiven for occasionally misconstruing this as an intimidating baring of teeth and threat of imminent attack. This has required us to provide rapid reassurance to passers-by on several occasions, as his glowing white teeth clash with the friendly wag of his tail. Anyway, the reason for this self-satisfied grin and obvious delight at how he spent his day, is that in Radar's eyes, the dog sitter's home represents a free stay in a den of debauchery and free love, with the prospect of a different girl every time. For the dog that is, not the owners – they are utterly respectable.

Unfortunately, his unrestrained adoration of all the female dogs did not go unnoticed and on collection, I was informed that he had had to be separated from his latest love interest with a warning that such behaviour may become 'a problem'. I'm interpreting this as a lightly veiled hint that he may no longer be welcome if his sex drive remains so out of control.

Aargh…what to do?

Surely you can't train a dog out of lust? It's not like I can sit down with him and explain the inappropriateness of his behaviour and promote the importance of a more respectful attitude towards his love interests. Is the only solution to follow the path of no return to castration? What if this changes his whole personality before he's fully developed, or leaves him fixed in an overgrown puppy mindset for life? Poor Radar.

Monday 28th November

Radar appears to be on a mission to recruit a backup team to safeguard his balls. Today this came in the form of dragging me into the path of a feisty older lady armed with two ferocious chihuahuas. This might appear to be a risky move for a dog intent on remaining as fully intact as possible, but with so much at stake he felt the risk was worth taking: This woman was After strategically lifting the most aggressive one into her arms, so that both Radar and I had to brave eye contact with at least one of these snarling midgets, she expressed her delight at seeing 'A *proper* pedigree dog' and embarked on a rant about the plague of trendy crossbreed designer dogs that would be out of fashion in no time. I smiled agreeably before we made our escape, still thankfully intact, as she retreated inside with her chihuahuas.

Unfortunately, despite such public approval of his breed, this encounter did not convince me that his breeding potential for pedigree progeny is worth preserving. I sense Radar's intact reprieve may be short-lived.

Friday 2nd December

 The dog's bollocks.

Why exactly are the dog's bollocks the ones that got lucky enough to be crowned with the testicular gold standard? I mean, why not an elephant – surely, they'd have something equally impressive to offer in this department?

For the anatomical nerds among you, I've just googled this and in case you hadn't noticed, elephants keep their testes well hidden inside and so perhaps that answers that one. What's more, this extensive research suggests that the winner of the award for the biggest balls is a toss-up between the tuberous bush cricket and the right whale, depending on which way you hang: The bush cricket possesses the largest known testes of any creature in relation to its body mass - a weighty 14% of the insect's body mass. To put this in context, if this was a bloke, his testicles would each weigh the equivalent of around six bags of sugar. Even as a woman, I'm currently feeling quite grateful not to be a male bush cricket. For anyone who is still reading this bollocks thesis, the right whale's testicles weigh in at 500 Kg each. So, still none the wiser as to why dog's snatch all the glory.

But back to the issue of Radar's virility. How did making this decision over what to do about the dog's bollocks become such a guilt trip? I'm sure that when we had dogs as a child, it was pretty much assumed and carried out with little debate or concern for the dog's ongoing mental development versus his potential to try to hump any abandoned blankets or Aunty Jane's leg.

Come to think of it, I do recall a particular childhood friend of mine causing my dog so much excitement and her some excruciating embarrassment, that he had to be locked away if she ever came round to hang out - so maybe we shouldn't overthink this.

The vet has been consulted on the dilemma of how to manage Radar's hormones and it turns out that there may be a third option as an alternative to a lifetime ban from the dog sitter's or having the chop – A hormone injection!

The beauty of this is that it isn't permanent but will give a good idea of how his behaviour and personality might alter if, at a later date, we were to choose the surgical option. Less positive is that it will cost more than the surgical alternative, will begin to wear off within a year and needs to be repeated if all concerned are to reap the benefits of more civilised behaviour.

The appointment has been booked, ensuring that

Aunty Jane et al. can sip tea in peace.

Friday 16th December

Injection day. £240 later and Radar has had the hormone injection that may help to calm his carnal desires. I'm not sure how long this may take to kick in but we have exactly four days before he next goes to spend some ~~time with~~ the dog sitter.

Monday 19th December

Quote of the day:

'Radar is a credit to you and your family'.

If I could put that up in lights I wouldn't hesitate.

This rare moment of praise came from the scary guru of impeccable dog behaviour who has been known to bestow spontaneous training sessions on us if we are lucky enough to cross paths whilst out walking.

All we need is for Radar to maintain this for a few more days...tomorrow he is die to spend his first day with the dog-sitter since he came close to receiving a lifetime ban.

Tuesday 20th December

I think the severity of Radar's predicament has sunk in. He has clearly realised that his future as a fully intact dog depends on convincing us that the injection was a great decision. To prove this, he spends the day being such delightful company at the dog sitter's, that he manages to not only fully redeem himself for his previous disreputable behaviour, but also rise back to the dizzy heights of their favourite dog. £240 well spent.

Phew.

A Dog's Christmas in Wales

Well, what can I say? Not one of the aforementioned adverts really summed up the experience of an extended family Christmas in Wales but here are a few useful pointers:

-        There is nothing like having a dog to take for a walk on the beach when you need to escape your kids/mother/husband/in-laws. If you are travelling to an area that is completely new to you, you can also legitimately justify getting lost.

- Should your dog just happen to feel compelled to repeatedly mark his territory on the footstall in the living room of the rental cottage, a suitably highly-scented cleaning spray should resolve the issue and discourage repeat performances. If this doesn't work, barricade yourself in the lounge alone and insist the others distract the dog elsewhere.

- Rest assured, that even if the unseasonably warm weather turns into an unexpected tempest, walking in gale force wind and pouring rain will be less painful than seeing your dog being bullied and forced to cower in a corner by your mother-in-law's vicious mutt. Even if this results in you losing the house key to the holiday home somewhere in the storm as you rummage in your pockets, blinded by sheets of rain, for poo bags.

- Dogs look fab in a cracker crown and can be impressively helpful in cleaning all the dishes.

Maybe next year I can be like Mrs Claus...

New Year's Day 2017

And so, the year has turned full course. That familiar New Year's Day feeling of mild nausea, a headache and lack of sleep is hitting hard, but this time we completely missed the party. Cruelly felled by a sudden bout of seasonal norovirus, I didn't have to worry about the hair of dog mixing with my velvet trousers, nor whether it was wiser to turn up to an Indian-themed evening in an inexpertly attached sari or a pair of harem pants accessorised with a top displaying a hungry Bengal tiger crawling across my chest. Not quite sure when I'll find the opportunity to wear either of these again but time will tell.

And yet all is not lost. Radar, in a way that only dogs know how, found a way to ensure I looked the part for the most important of New Year's Day traditions – the long post-hangover walk. Generously willing to overlook my lack of genuine hangover, Radar reassured me that the important thing is just to get outside, pull on my newly gifted waxed jacket and blow away those pesky viruses.

Where does this dog get his ideas about public health?

I humoured him.

More likely, he was having the real laugh on my behalf.

By the time we left the house, the weather had turned distinctly showery and I was dressed from head-to-toe as a cliché of a rural Labrador owner. Chunky greenish wellies, practical wax jacket and to cap it all I'd even grabbed Doug's broad brimmed waterproof hat. Radar seemed suitably satisfied with my attire until we reached the furthest, wettest and muddiest point from home, at which point, as I stashed his favourite filthy ball in my pocket, he went into full retriever mode. Repeatedly, he leapt up, covering me from head to toe in mud, pretending to try to get his toy back but quite clearly disgusted at the overly pristine state of my coat. He didn't quit until we reached civilisation once more, at which point he resumed the role of the faithful dog, whilst leaving me looking like I'd been sleeping rough in ditch. He had of course saved me from one of the greatest fashion faux pas of wax jacket wearing - it should never look like you never wear it. It took a few cups of tea and a couple of dark chocolate cookies to grudgingly acknowledge the favour he'd done me. All is (almost) forgiven.

Wednesday 4th January

Armed with a stylishly wrecked coat and a healthy dose of post-virus hallucination, I am confident that this fresh new year is going to be a breeze on the dog-parenting front.

Just to strategically reinforce this point, Radar has been impeccable for the entirety of the last four days. Clearly, he is a changed dog and we are now well on the path to regaining control of both our dog and our lives.

Perhaps having a dog isn't so bad after all.

Thursday 5th January

...Or perhaps, he was just holding out until his birthday.

Today, Radar turns one!

Whilst my human children have, over the years, chosen to show a diverse range of behaviours on their birthdays, ranging from being charming hosts to self-centred and overwrought mini-dictators, with the dog things were looking more straightforward. For him, a birthday was the perfect opportunity to show off his newfound maturity and impeccable breeding.

With panache, he demonstrated perfect recall from his experience over Christmas, on how to rip and shred the paper off gifts and play delightedly with whatever he discovered on the inside.

Such a talented boy!

Never, in my time as a parent, has every carefully wrapped present been so gratefully received and focussed on to the exclusion of all others for quite so long. So long in fact, that getting through the modest pile of gifts took over an hour, with us ultimately having to distract him from each in turn and then hide every gift before moving onto the next. This proved to be a very entertaining game for Radar and a complete failure for us, as he doggedly sniffed out and retrieved all gifts with impressive skill.

And then there was the meaty dog cake for tea, which he didn't have to share with anyone. Thank goodness. Imagine having to politely tuck into a slice of meaty dog food covered in some sort of suety paste? No. Don't imagine that. Revolting.

On the plus side, he didn't require candles as he hasn't yet learned to blow. Phew! The thought of a combo involving flaming candles and a cake-hungry Labrador ends badly whichever way you cut it.

To cap it all, we presented him with a brand new bed as he seems to have reached his full size. At least I hope he's reached his full size - he is already taller and longer than every other Labrador we meet. I guess this is what happens when you pick the greediest guzzler of the litter.

Friday 6th January

There is nothing like a new year for getting back into shape with a good run followed up with a counterproductive hot coffee and a chocolate brownie with a friend; and there is also nothing quite like having a dog bring you right back down to earth with a bang for daring to indulge so blatantly.

'I think Radar might have found something…' was the polite but slightly restrained comment from my friend.

'…Maybe a tissue?' she adds helpfully.

I wonder what Radar could possibly have retrieved this time, after his rip-roaring show of talent yesterday.

It turns out that yesterday was just a gentle birthday preamble.

Radar has just entered the room with his mouth full of what to me is very clearly a used sanitary towel.

Ok, I'm sorry if you were also enjoying a lovely coffee and cake whilst reading this, but this is exactly the sort of scenario a dog-parent might have to deal with and there really is no point sugar-coating it.

I have no idea where or how he could have got hold of such a thing, other than having somehow evaded my husband, snuck upstairs, raided a bathroom bin and then chosen that exact moment to share his trawl. For obvious reasons, I wasn't going to spend more than a millisecond over-thinking this and leapt up to discreetly retrieve the 'tissue'.

Radar however was typically alert to my every move, and *so* delighted with his find that he took to holding out in a secure position under the kitchen table. Reduced to my hands and knees, I joined him there as we entered into a less-than-becoming game of chase. I like to think that ultimately, I won, but I suspect that I was just a pawn in his game, playing entirely to Radar's rules.

My friend, probably still grateful from being saved from the fate of dog ownership after her close shave last year, remained tight-lipped on the matter, no doubt suitably distracted by her brownie, which *was* sugar-coated. A delicate dusting of icing sugar in case you were wondering.

Saturday January 7th

Radar has clearly been on some sort of tail wagging charm offensive. Somehow, he has managed to get himself an invitation to spend the day on an exclusive shoot that would normally have required social connections way beyond our circle. I thought we had escaped this possibility by avoiding the main haunts of the sausage roll crowd, but it seems Radar has somehow won them round from afar. This is madness. Quite why any self-respecting shoot enthusiast would be prepared to risk their expedition with as overly excitable a dog as Radar is quite beyond me - surely this has the potential to end badly for all concerned? Apart from the pheasants perhaps. They would get wind of his arrival within moments and initiate an immediate evacuation on the surrounding woods.

Just the thought of the potential chaos is causing me to have panicked visions of a wild ~~goose~~ pheasant chase; guns and beaters all in tow as feathers fly and Radar makes off by diving for cover in one of the Land Rovers and absconding with the sausage rolls.

This alone is enough to stop me from spending too much time mulling over the moral question of a shoot-to-kill dining policy versus the low carbon footprint potential of a field to table dinner, alongside the additional dilemma of allowing Radar the joy of fulfilling what he was bred to do versus loafing in front of the fire all day. The slight twang of guilt I feel at not indulging his heritage, is quickly put to bed by imagining the double trouble I'd be in with The Gamekeeper if Radar got a taste for this activity.

The balance being clearly-tipped, I decline the

invitation. There is no way I'm spending the day standing in a muddy field on a bitterly cold January day, with a dog who I'm sure is more inclined to join the beater's spaniels in scaring pheasants from the undergrowth, rather than reliably retrieving fallen fowl.

Thursday 12th January

Snow!

Visions of the Radar frolicking excitedly and photogenically in virgin powder have been filling my imagination since the forecast last night. I had also been hoping it might hit early and give us that glorious gift of a snow day from school.

This however wasn't quite how it panned out.

The reality was that the snow showed no sign of arriving in time to prevent the morning commute, instead saving itself for the end of the day. As such, I got home late from work after a meeting, having driven through a ferocious blizzard to an un-walked dog, cold damp sleet and impending darkness. On finally heading for the hills, the wind was so strong that it blew my hat off. On a brighter note, Radar finds this turn of events so exciting that he races off to retrieve it and returns it proudly but reluctantly with a generous coating of slobber and mud.

Perhaps he has the instincts of a talented retriever after all?

Or more likely, this was a vengeful ruse for my turning down his invitation to share sausages with the local elite and prove his worth in the field with far more exciting quarry than my hat.

Saturday 14th January

Another day, and another overly enthusiastic greeting by Radar of a couple and their large dog. Unsure who to greet first, he went for a cover-all approach and followed his spin and sniff of their dog with a leap up towards its owners.

I immediately offer profuse apologies whilst attempting to bring him back into line, but it appears that they weren't in the least perturbed by the nature of his greeting, declaring themselves to be 'Dog People'.

Is there a chance that I might finally be becoming a Dog Person?

Can one become a Dog Person, or is it innate?

Perhaps I am a trainee Dog Person?

Or a half-Dog Person? …No, that sounds weird.

Enough philosophical musing for today.

Sunday 15th January

One of my oldest friends made an impromptu visit today, hoping, I think, to meet Radar for only the second time and in doing so, reinforce her conviction that they too would enjoy having a dog in the family.

I wonder fleetingly whether she has chosen the right household to achieve this and reminisce a little on the first time we introduced her family to Radar.

On that occasion, we met for an idyllic walk on the Stockbridge water meadows, followed up with the suggestion by her husband of grabbing a swift pint in the local pub. As compelling as this suggestion sounded, I was inwardly looking aghast and feeling a rising sense of panic at the prospect of taking our crowd of four adults, 5 children and a puppy, into the bar; but, not wanting to spoil the party, I faked an enthusiastic smile, and hoped that a drink might soothe any accompanying trauma.

This might have all gone well if the establishment hadn't been quite *so* dog friendly. However, faced with room full of intoxicating cooking smells and friendly looking pooches at every other table, Radar could not sit still. Neither could he sit quietly, as he experimented with repeated volleys of piercing barks to express his frustration. We lasted less than seven minutes before the 'swift' pint became a swift exit.

All credit to the optimistic nature of my friend, but by today's visit, she seemed to have entirely put this earlier episode behind her – after all, this was months ago and surely no indicator of what life with a dog was really going to be like. Obviously, I shared a blunt and honest description of how dog ownership had felt over the last year, but my words fell on deaf ears. Neither tripping in the dog's paw-crafted muddy bunkers in the grass, nor the cold and over stewed cups of tea that were left abandoned as we were distracted by a trail of a shredded boar treat bag, made even the slightest bit of difference. The lenses of her rose-tinted glasses were tattooed with images of her perfect fantasy Whippet, and nothing was going to change that.

To be fair, apart from the episode with the boar treats, Radar didn't show himself up at all this-afternoon. In fact, I would go as far as to say that he was beginning to show tendencies towards civilised behaviour. My case was falling apart.

Of course, once they had said their goodbyes and headed home after a delightful afternoon in his company, Radar relaxed his guard returning to his preferred theme of the week:

'Getting the Upper Paw'

Throughout this week he has once again started leaping up at me wildly on our walks, including once in the middle of the village to ensure his spectacle was available to be freely enjoyed by all passing traffic, like some sort of spontaneous drive-in movie.

At this point I am beginning to wonder if we are making any progress at all. I have no idea why this behaviour has once again raised its head, but I am really frustrated that I might have to endure this again. I was so sure we'd got through this.

Monday 16th January

This morning started exactly as it should have done for the third Monday in January. Pitch black, a biting drizzle, a mud bath walk, and all before I could even think about getting dressed for work.

I am at this point wondering why I get the pleasure of full exposure to 'Blue Monday' while the rest of the household lie in bed, and I can categorically assure you that this is because teenagers have cleverly evolved to outstrip their parents and as such would not be foolish enough to indulge in such excursions at this ungodly hour on a Monday morning in January. Doug has a get-out-of-ungodly-walks free card as he wakes up so stiff from his back condition that early morning races up hills are still not on the agenda. I can only advise any future dog-parents out there to subscribe the same school of thought as their offspring.

And I genuinely wish you the very best of luck with that.

Of course, there is always the afternoon excursion to look forward to. No leaping out of bed for that one, and at this time of year it comes in multiple shades of grey any time from 3.30 onwards and today certainly doesn't disappoint on that front. By 4pm the dog is desperate to explore this monochrome world and yet the bl***y lead is missing. AGAIN.

As Radar expresses his impatience with increasingly voluble whimpers, I search high and low, covering every surface, every room, even in the cars and the garden but to no avail.

Eventually, as the dog's desperation reaches fever pitch, the lead reveals itself under the laundry basket.

How could this be?

Did someone *actually* move some laundry while I was out?

Surely not?

This grand reveal did not however take place before I'd traipsed muddy wellies in and out of the house multiple times in an attempt to speed up my search. More competent dog-parents out there might of course have had the presence of mind to remove said wellies before coming in, but, in my defence, I had indulgently put on a pair of cosy and therefore rather thick, welly socks. 'Cosy' is in fact not really a strong enough word for the boot/sock combo, as once on, the boots fitted so snugly that removing them would have required the pulling power of an Olympian turnip tugging team, and unfortunately, in that moment they just weren't available. Perhaps on our return, as a special Blue Monday treat, I'll let the dog traipse a further field's worth of mud through the house to make the clean-up feel like a genuinely worthwhile experience.

Friday 20th January

Warning: Changing your dog's food can have a detrimental effect on the contents of his stomach.

I guess this should have been obvious, but I can assure you that the sheer size and frequency of his excretions in the last 24 hours defy belief.

Dietary changes should not be taken lightly. I shall say no more on this matter.

Saturday 21st January

Actually – scrap that. As of 7 am this-morning, I have a LOT more to say on this matter.

In a moment of weakness, in the light of this bitterly cold January morning, it seemed preferable not to bother with our usual early morning trip to the field, and so, throwing caution to the wind, I blithely opened the back door and let him out to wreck the lawn at will, concluding that it was a small price to pay for the rare treat of a lazy start with a couple of coffees.

At least it would have been a small price, if it hadn't been for the small and overlooked detail of the food changes. How could I have possibly overlooked this less than 24 hours after yesterday's unmentionable incident? The truth is that I really thought we were through the worst.

Not so.

No longer was Radar depositing a straightforward solid pile, or even a solitary over-sized one. That would have been far too easy. This-morning's variation was for him to once again leap from patch to patch, depositing seven or more sloppy, sticky piles of mess. To keep track of the location of each, whilst simultaneously identifying where the next would land, would have required a photographic memory alongside the skills of a talented minesweeper to retrieve all deposits without incident.

Momentarily, my inner nerd pondered the benefits of putting on my son's night vision goggles to locate the deposits. Admittedly, it wasn't exactly dark, but I had a vague notion that they work on thermal radiation and so could potentially make the task exceptionally straightforward.

Perhaps I should google this theory.

Or perhaps not.

Mercifully, some deeply buried glimmer of self-preservation in the street cred department glares at me, aghast. And so, contritely, I decide that the thought of having to explain, or worse, not finding the opportunity to explain to any passing observers, why I was wandering across my lawn at dawn in night vision goggles and picking up poo, was a step too far even for me. Besides, it was bl***y freezing and by this point I was damn sure that any thermal energy was rapidly dissipating. Consoling myself with the thought that frozen poo might be easier to pick up and far less problematic if accidentally stepped in I head indoors.

The weather might not have improved as the day progressed, but by lunch time, I had experienced a glimmer of a silver lining to this bitterly brown tinged and odorous cloud. This breakthrough came about unexpectedly as I found myself wandering through a local garden centre killing time during my son's tennis lesson. Garden centres, and in fact gardening are not perhaps the most exciting places in January, unless cut price Christmas decorations are your thing, but unbeknownst to me, this branch had a hidden gem – A PET STORE!

Stumbling across this delight in my slightly glum and semi-frostbitten state was the highlight of my day, though not so perhaps for the assistant who was unfortunate enough to now be my captive audience. Perhaps he'd had a quiet morning until this point, but never have I met anyone who seemed so genuinely fascinated by my tales of woe at our latest choice of dog food. With surprising enthusiasm, he nodded knowingly as I detailed Radar's bowel habits, sparing him no details, before bounding across to the food section to recommend another brand that would surely see an end to my troubles.

Such was the power of his sales technique, that I delightedly purchased a large sack of the recommended food, even though it was even higher in protein than the original variety that we had abandoned for the one that caused all the bowel issues. Still, this was just a minor detail and one that I was suitably distracted from as I found myself inexplicably hypnotised by the dark eyes of a life-sized plastic Labrador sat on the shelves of 'garden' ornaments...perhaps in another life one of those would have been a simpler choice...

Saturday 28th January

On a positive note, it turns out that the pet shop assistant was not only a welcome ear to bend, shoulder to cry on (metaphorically of course, I do have some capacity to hold it together) and superb salesman, but he was also clearly a guru dog-dietician. Ever since our visit, Radar's bowels are back to normal!

Unfortunately, the same cannot be said of his boisterous behaviour which has taken a worrying nosedive. His leaping up randomly on walks with Sascha or me has really escalated and although it isn't exactly an attack, it feels aggressive and hard to control, like a game that has the capacity to go very wrong, very quickly. We are all beginning to feel increasingly desperate to resolve this and so Doug suggests that maybe the dog needs to be seen by a dog psychologist.

Hmmm…exactly how would this work?

They can hardly sit down with him and talk things through, can they?

You know what? I'm in no position to overthink this. At this point it feels like anything is worth a shot and throwing any reservations to one side, I'm beginning to think that Doug has a point. The only thing is the price tag - at £250 for a morning's consultation, this isn't to be taken lightly, but the situation is becoming critical. The psychologist has assured us that he can usually resolve an issue like this within one session. This would be nothing short of miraculous, but first the dog has to play ball and show his worst side when they come to work with him. This is far from guaranteed. He is more likely to see their game and roll on his back with his legs in the air and charm them into believing he's an angel.

Wednesday 1st February

Today I have been off work sick. Plagued with a heavy cold and stomach pains, all dog duties have had to be handed over to my in-house emergency back-up team, and as such, the dog is looking very hard done by.

You might have thought that under the circumstances, Radar would have been quite appreciative of Sascha returning by late afternoon to give him a decent walk. Sadly, not so.

Any glimmer of gratitude was heavily outweighed by the dog being possessed by dangerous levels of pent-up energy and within minutes of leaving the house, Sascha rings me in dire straits, declaring that Radar has gone nuts and she needs immediate back-up. He has spontaneously switched into his alter ego of a crazy dog, leaping at her aggressively and not letting up. I jump off my sick bed, grab the nearest footwear (just polished boots but at this point who cares) and try to run for the hills... Well, the hill, singular. I'm haven't quite reached the point of abandoning the ship and its increasingly desperate crew just yet. By the time I arrive, Sascha has managed to gain the upper hand and whilst both are caked in mud from top to toe, Radar has recovered from his moment of madness and is wondering what all the fuss was about. Sascha and I however, are not in such good shape and at this point I have no idea what to do.

Where on earth have we gone wrong?

Can I even trust him to be left with the kids or even the dog sitter?

Do we really need a dog psychologist?

WHY ME????

Thursday 2nd February

Suddenly, as if by magic, the dog-sitter appeared! *

(*For those readers old enough to have also experienced a British 1970's childhood and therefore familiar with a similarly magical utterance by Mr Ben proclaiming the repeatedly miraculous appearance of that fancy dress shop owner, the perfectly timed coincidence of the dog-sitter in our midst was a similarly heady gift of reassuring tones and the thrill of possibilities about to unfold. This has absolutely nothing to do with me verging on being delirious with stress at Radar's behaviour and heading for a breakdown in the form of reverting to childhood heroes to get me through this.)

Or for those of every other generation, just as we were beginning to lose our way, in came Shuna, Radar's favourite dog-sitter and trainer, who, on hearing of our current predicament, bravely offered to take him on and train him out of it. What she'll really be doing is training *us* out of it - as with parenting, so with dog-rearing - apparently, it's all about the adults. Still, at this point, I'm so relieved that I'll take anything. This will mean weekly classes on Saturday mornings, come rain or shine, covering all sorts of inappropriate dog and owner behaviour. This wasn't how I had hoped to be spending my weekends, but not only did it mean we were hopefully going to find a way out of this, but as Shuna knows Radar so well, there really was no one better placed to assist.

Perhaps sensing that this might be the right moment to casually throw in some less positive news, she also mentions that Radar has been showing a rather passionate interest in Kora – a similarly aged Lab belonging to the landowners of the local shoot. On the surface, this could be a worrying development - perhaps the hormone injection is only lightly holding back his desire? But on calm reflection, due to the sedative effects of the training offer, I conclude it has nothing to do with hormones, and everything to do with his stomach – Kora's owner is also the baker of the divine sausage rolls which Radar would undoubtedly bypass her dog for every day of the week. No offence Kora, but as a fellow Labrador, I'm sure you'll understand where his priorities lie.

Friday 10th February

Ever since we have booked Radar in for training with Shuna, his behaviour has been impeccable. I have no idea what Radar's game plan is here or what on earth to think.

I can't cancel as this needs to be sorted, but how do you train a dog out of bad behaviour if is he isn't exhibiting any bad behaviour?

Surely, we shouldn't be encouraging the crazy episodes just to get him out of them?!? This is proving even harder than raising children.

Friday 17th February

So, once again, tomorrow is DT (Dog training) day. I find myself wondering whether it is any coincidence that DT is also the acronym that we use in school for a detention?

Not sure if it is me or the dog who is in more trouble here, but on the upside, last week's training related dilemma has been resolved by a distinct downturn in behaviour. With impeccable timing, Radar has resumed his moments of frenzied leaping, inexplicably demonstrating this at exactly the same point at the brow of the hill on the return leg of each walk.

Saturday 18th February

As DT's go, the morning's dog-training went pretty much as planned. Or perhaps that should read, exactly as Radar planned.

Radar and I turned up on time and spent an

hour being put through our paces as he duly demonstrated the best of his behaviour at the required moment, with only the slightest of passing nods to his alter ego of monster dog before quickly remembering his mission to maintain cover as an adorable and exceptional Labrador. Shuna observed with interest and within a split second of any digressions, Radar stepped back from the brink of monstrosity to resume his normal charm offensive. So far, so good, and we were sent home with some exercises to practice on our walks and the suggestion that we should do our best to ignore any bad behaviour and reward the good. This was comfortingly familiar, resonating with the contemporary wisdom on child-rearing, and so, somewhat reassured, I resolved to test out this strategy at the first opportunity. We headed home with tails slightly less between our legs and even with a daring hint of a wag.

That is, until we embarked on the afternoon walk.

The moment we hit the danger point of the retreat down the hill, Radar, perfectly on cue, leapt into action. Ruthlessly focussed on testing my ability to follow this-morning's instructions, he used every trick in his dog-eared book to get my attention. I countered by attempting to ignore and turn away from his every move. From initially trying to get to my arm as I turned away from him in a futile attempt to ignore his advance, he added barking, leaping and finally growling to his repertoire. Like the arms race (no pun intended on the arm issue), he just wouldn't quit. To him this variation of behaviour was just another version of the game, and neither of us was prepared to lose. But the situation was getting worse. The onslaught progressed for what might have been seconds but felt like several very long and increasingly painful minutes; and so, very quickly, I was forced to regain control before the situation got completely out of hand. A melting pot of frustration, disappointment, distress and shock, I could barely get off the hill and home without completely breaking down, and in that moment, If I'm honest, I was truly regretting the day we got him.

The whole family could see that something was seriously wrong the moment we traipsed through the door. Radar retreated to his bed, full of obvious shame, but this had come too late. I was shell-shocked and utterly demoralised, covered in mud and my arm was in pain, and likely to be seriously bruised. None of us knew what to do or say. I felt utterly trapped, with no clear way out.

I am putting every ounce of energy into trying to make this work, whilst also compensating for my husband's lack of capacity due to his health problems and my children's typically teenage reluctance to over-exert themselves. I feel as if I haven't got a lot more to give. Biting my tongue to prevent myself from pointlessly screaming 'I TOLD

YOU SO' from the rooftops offered little salve.

And yet if we can't find a way through this what do we do?

Is it possible to train him out of this or is he irreparably dangerous? Do we admit defeat? If so, what does that even mean? Could he even be rehomed? Would he be regarded as so dangerous that we have him put down? I can barely even put these possibilities into words, because at the end of the day, despite what seems to be an insurmountable challenge, he is still one of the family and there would be no victory in concluding that we were wrong to take on a dog - it would simply be devasting.

Doug would lose his much-loved canine companion and personal trainer. Sascha would lose her beloved confidant and friend in times of need, and even Charlie, who has never really got over the death of our cat a few years back, has grown very fond of Radar and is completely confused as to how his dog can behave so differently when on walks with me.

The only cure-all that I can come up with, is to find the strength to manage his behaviour and train him out of it. This feels like an Everest to climb. But I am tired and upset. I could really do with more help and yet every request feels dismissed and fought against. Whilst on a deeper level I know that everyone is doing their best, I'm not feeling this right now. This is not what I signed up for and yet I'm rapidly realising that I'm the only one who can get us out of this.

DAMN IT.

I cast a glance at his sad and guilt-ridden eyes as he lies, ears tentatively pricked to the horrors of the jeopardy he is in, and despite the emotional trauma of the afternoon, my heart still melts.

And then, as I wince whilst pulling a jumper over my rapidly bruising and tender arm, I'm momentarily reminded of my friend who took on an even greater challenge. The one who had to dress her family in luminous jackets around the house to support their rescue dog in his fear of workmen. Or the fact that she had to give up her job to be there for him. This might seem extreme, but it serves its purpose as a sharp but timely reminder that perhaps I'm being a bit of a wimp.

Besides, I'm not actually that good at quitting.

At this point though, Radar's future still hovers dangerously in the balance, and the plan is nothing more than a glimmer of hope.

But then, as if to nudge me further along this uphill path and reinforce my resolution, my phone pings with a reassuring check-in from our fairy ~~dog~~ godmother, Shuna:

"How are things? Did Radar behave on his walk this-afternoon?"

Confession time.

With a poorly faked air of calm, I explain exactly *how* wrong the experiment in ignoring his behaviour went.

"I think I might have taken your advice a little too literally" I shamefully admit, before launching into a vivid description of the clash of wills Radar and I had undergone.

Like all good fairy godmothers, with a swish of her wand, a sprinkle of reassurance headed down the line. (OK - I couldn't *actually* see her wand as this was long before dog training could be done via Zoom calls*, but it was undoubtedly swishing and wagging like an ecstatic Labrador's tail.)

"You're not alone in this, Julia." She kindly pointed out. "How about I come for a walk with you and Radar tomorrow evening and we watch him in action together?"

At this point, I could have fallen on my knees with gratitude. Tomorrow is another day and that tiny spark of hope is glowing gently.

*I lie. It still can't. Dog training will never be done by video conferencing. Don't let's even think about such a ridiculous proposition. Any dog worth his kind would never consent to such a charade. It would be like learning to sniff out abandoned tennis balls by making your dog watch the Wimbledon highlights. Please don't correct me on this - I have my fingers in my ears and am humming very loudly.

Monday 20th February

After yesterday's events, Charlie and I have decided to abscond. Not permanently of course, or even for long enough to miss this-evening's training expedition with Shuna, but a bit of distance between myself and the problem is just what this weary dog-mother has ordered. And so today, dog-free, we are heading off for some motherly and grandmotherly TLC. And tea. And cake. Large amounts of it.

Resolving to keep things light, I don a long-sleeved top so as not to attract attention to the bruised arm and worry my mum.

Unfortunately, such was my elation at a Duty Free day (gosh, that sounds revitalising on a couple of counts...) that I forgot to include Charlie in the 'No Comment on the Dog' policy.

Within seconds of our arrival he had let the cat out of the bag *and* the dog out of the doghouse, causing a chaotic conversational cat and dog chase that tipped a couple of duty-free glasses right up the wrong way. Still, empowered with a few remaining glimmers of yesterday's fairy dust, I managed to cast a sprinkling of convincing reassurances that I had the situation COMPLETELY UNDER CONTROL.

This involved buoyant descriptions of the top-quality training regime that we were going to undertake and then, to really put my mother at ease, I told her how we were also going to employ the services of a highly regarded dog psychologist to ensure we had dotted every 'i' and crossed every 't' in the dog training canon.

Titititititititititititititititiiitit.

Sorry. I'm being silly. Clearly a day with my mother is bringing out my inner child. It has also clearly brought out my inner idiot, as I had thrown in the dog psychologist comment without a backward, sideways, or forward glance, or even the slightest expectation that she would be so full of admiration at our thorough approach to dog-rearing. Perhaps I should have realised that anything that might protect her daughter and grandchildren was unlikely to fall on deaf ears, but as a result, I have now inadvertently committed us to going through with this extortionate backup policy.

Oh well, in for a penny, in for a pound. A monetary pound (plural); NOT a dog pound (singular). Obviously. Somehow or other, we are going to have to crack this.

The moment I get home, and before I have the time to talk myself out of it, I pick up the phone and ring the dog psychologist. It clicks to answerphone. Resolute, I leave a message, and head out with Shuna to walk the dog and await his worst.

Radar, to his credit, has never let Shuna down in the training department. That is something he saves almost exclusively for me at my most vulnerable, and so, I can see that having the two of us to play off at the same time must have messed with his head big time. He expresses this by putting on an impressively mercurial performance.

Before we even get to the hill, Radar is greeted rather aggressively by a large Doberman, but, rather than launch into a defensive pseudo-monster attack, he simply rolls on his back and lets the beast sniff his balls. This stark contrast to his brave and boisterous leaps at me can only mean that I figure lower than a flea in terms of the level of threat I must represent to him. Under the circumstances, this is in no way comforting. Should I develop a terrifying alter ego to parallel a feisty Doberman or play it safe and roll on my back every time he launches himself at me?

Before getting very far with this train of thought, Shuna brutally intercepts my reverie

"That dog is a menace!" she announces with conviction.

I follow her eyes in the middle distance and realise that her disdain is not focussed on Radar but on the retreating figure of the cocky Doberman.

"I have never seen Radar so submissive" she muses.

Part of me is delighted to have the 'naughty dog' label focussed momentarily on a different mutt, but, between you and me, I think Radar has just put on an Oscar worthy performance entirely for her benefit and wonder what he has planned next.

We do not have to wait long.

The brow of the hill is within reach, and I can sense he is considering his next move. Like a chess grandmaster he assesses the battlefield. To his left, I stroll casually, a mere pawn in his game, ready to be leapt upon and sacrificed for the greater good at any moment; to his right strides Shuna, the Queen of Canines, an altogether different challenge. But what a victory it would be to take her down! I watch, trying to gauge which way the battle will go. Radar bides his time, assessing the position of any outlying players. As we turn the corner into open country, it is clear that there are no outsiders within reach. And that is when he makes his move. The pawn can wait her turn. He leaps for the Queen. Unperturbed, she stares him down and he retreats. Risking everything, he makes a second attempt, but once again is crushed by the stealth and experience of his opponent. He steps back accepting the precarious nature of his position. He may have exhibited his prowess on the field, but he has sacrificed his advantage over the Queen. His game plan has been exposed and counter strategies will now be imposed. Concluding that a low profile is the best cover, Radar reverts to being a loving and loyal Labrador, trotting nicely by our sides for the whole trip home and politely accepting treats for his trouble.

I suspect that he thinks we will forget all about his misdemeanours now that he has put on such a show, but little does he know what tricks Shuna has stuffed up my sleeve to pull out and counter his every move.

The chess board will be thrown in the air and replaced with a far more effective distraction – a squeaky toy! Try to put aside any doubts on this – I can assure you that there is nothing more powerful in the armoury of dog versus man as a distracting squeak in your pocket.

What's more, in a strategy of *supreme* genius, the route we walk is to be turned on its head: Radar's habitual point of attack will thereby be avoided on every return journey. Ha! This is a plan of such simplicity, I can't believe I didn't think of it myself.

We will of course be continuing with weekly training sessions covering all the bases to ensure ~~he is~~ we are thoroughly transformed into always behaving impeccably.

Not to mention the bank-breaking back-up plan of the dog psychologist.

Friday 24th February

To reward his surrender to the Queen, Radar has earned himself a whole weekend of doggy debauchery in her home. What's more, as an extra special treat, he will be enjoying the company of fellow guest, Kora, the very posh Labrador who he loves unconditionally for her impeccable sausage roll connections.

We, however, have a less exciting weekend ahead and will be heading down to Wales to visit my mother-in-law and attend another family funeral.

Such events are of course bleak at the best of times, but this hasn't been the easiest of weeks and it is about to get worse. As we gather together with my parents-in-law over dinner, an accidental reveal of the now mottled shades of black and blue up my left arm as I absent-mindedly adjusted my attire to accommodate their tropically heated home, did nothing to improve the direction of the conversation.

"You can't let a dog get the better of you like that!" my mother-in-law helpfully suggests.

Damn – why didn't I think of that?

I quell my irritation and wonder if she will follow up with a gem of training wisdom honed through generations of rescue dog experience that might save us from any further distress, but her next comment is directed at her son.

"These are the sorts of issues that can really affect relationships - I hope you're not letting this dog come between the two of you?"

Whilst this is clearly intended as a caring pointer, the problem is that it hits a very sensitive nerve.

Neither of us really know how to respond, because if I'm honest, things are pretty tough in that department right now. I can almost see the phrase 'It's me or the dog' silently ricocheting between all parties in the room, but deep down, I know that this is not the root of the problem.

The trauma of the last couple of years of my husband's illness, job loss and pain have been life-changing for us all, but particularly for him. I feel like I'm just waiting for the storm to pass, whilst marching on with my head down against a raging torrent of challenges and moods But I also feel him slipping away from me emotionally and the trials and tribulations with the dog are just a small part of the picture.

Maybe Radar senses this and is trying to test my mettle and prove myself as a suitable pack-leader? Personally, I can think of better ways than simply trying to take me down and might have to discuss this with him at the first opportunity.

Sunday 26th February

Radar of course has had a fabulous weekend and has returned with a glowing report of impeccable behaviour and a healthy glow to his cheeks. He looks very pleased with himself on both counts.

Saturday 4th March

We have officially been dog parents for an entire year! This time last year we were bringing home our pup for the first time, completely clueless as to what fun and games he would drag us into. I have no idea what the next few months and years might hold but I am reminded of the comments from one of my children's' music teachers who I bumped into in the Aldi car park during those early, slightly headier days of new-puppydom.

"It will get so much easier in a couple of years", she reassured me as I recounted the experiences of our first two weeks.

"A couple of years!?" I spluttered, visibly shaken.

Only the day before, someone had told me the first six months were the worst. That had seemed reasonable, but two years?

Now, with the acquired wisdom of a 12-monther, I realise she was absolutely on the nose -this journey has only just begun and with a dog like Radar I think we might be barely off the starting blocks.

Thursday 9th March

It's totally reasonable to talk to your dog, right? I mean, I'm pretty sure that one of their most important functions is to listen to us silently and without judgement?

It was with this is mind, that I casually mentioned to Radar that the best way to win me over, keep my spirits high and my energy buoyant was to guard the household supply of cake with his life and ensure that there is always a slice left for me. I pointed out that this applies particularly to chocolate cake. Exceptions might occasionally be made for fruit cake, which isn't nearly so valuable.

He looked like he understood this concept and I would even go so far as to say that he was ready to put this into action at the first opportunity for the sake of my general well-being. The deal was struck.

And so it was that this very afternoon, unbeknownst to me, Radar would find himself presented with the challenge of a lifetime: A freshly baked triple layer chocolate Oreo cake to guard, that had been baked by my daughter in time for her Duke of Edinburgh award skill assessment later that evening.

This important task had completely passed me by until I finally returned home at 6.59pm – one minute before they were due to leave for the presentation of the cake.

Unfortunately, in the preceding minutes, Radar, who had dutifully had his beady eyes fixed on the cake during the entire construction process, concluded that as Sascha turned her back to seek out a cake tin, he needed to get closer to the cake to ensure that it was safe in her absence.

Little did any of us know, that Radar was absolutely right that the cake was in terrible danger. Covering the entire cake was a thick coating of brown, chocolate icing thickened with enormous quantities of butter and lard.

I suspect that it was the overpowering scent of the lard that in the heat of the moment, broke all of Radar's defences. This cake looked and *almost* smelled like his birthday cake. Eight long weeks may have passed but the smell was undeniably familiar. Surely this was something meant for him? In a flash his tongue was taste-testing the icing and a split second later, Sascha turned around in abject horror at the scene in front of her.

This was the point at which I walked through the front door.

An air of frenzied panic and fraught shrieks were emerging from the kitchen. Radar was nowhere to be seen and icing was being removed from the entire side of the cake and rapidly replaced with scavenged leftovers and a smearing from the untouched half.

Minutes later Doug and Sascha left the house with a vaguely presentable construction, declaring loudly that I needed to contact the emergency vet IMMEDIATELY as the icing was mixed up with half a tonne of cocoa powder which can be fatal for dogs.

I am left with a scene of utter destruction in the kitchen with ingredients, pans and fatty smears of icing on every surface and somewhere in the house, a guilty and potentially poisoned dog.

I ring the vet.

No doubt he had just returned from a full day at the surgery when he picked up my message about possibly chocolate consumption, but he returned my call within minutes. Yet again I am eternally grateful for his understanding, calm approach. He reassured me that the quantity of cocoa licked would have been minimal especially as it was mixed up with all that fat and so no need to panic about Radar's well-being.

On the other hand, he did offer some general advice about the risks of having chocolate in the house with a dog. He suggested that the best strategy would be to not keep dark chocolate in the house at all. Part of me was beginning to zone out in panic at this point – with no chocolate reserve, can I function as a normal human being? I manage to thank him for his advice and am hugely relieved that the dog is OK but I have no idea how to manage the chocolate situation. I'm thinking high cupboards and a lockable vault…

You'll be pleased to know that the cake assessment was passed with flying colours.

Saturday 11th March

I am now absolutely sure that I have come across the most helpful and knowledgeable pet-shop employee on the planet. This is the guy who just a few weeks ago, recommended that bowel-improving and life-changing pet food. Life-changing for me that is, not the dog - he really didn't give a sh**, or sometimes he gave too many, but that's all by the by. Today, as I browsed for some tasty and additive free treats, the same shop assistant came across and talked me through the entire range before we settled on a duck flavoured chew that could be cut to size according to your needs. Brilliant! It was only as I remembered that I needed to stock up on some of the green, super strong poo bags that I had bought from him last time, that I saw his face shift into an expression of genuine concern. For a moment I was worried that I'd given him the wrong idea and implied that his food recommendation hadn't worked, but fortunately this was not the case.

"I'm really sorry madam, but the green ones are completely out of stock." he commiserated. "But we do have them in sea blue… or, my particular favourite – lime green with a paw print design!"

Clearly still a complete sucker for an enthusiastic and emotionally laden sales pitch, I pocketed a packet of each to ensure I could pick and mix to match my mood in the coming weeks.

Never did I imagine that buying duck treats and poo bags could bring so much joy to two people.

Wednesday 15th March

Booster vaccine day. That annual event that fills every dog with dread, and, if I'm honest, after cake-gate last week, part of me is not quite so keen to face the vet either. It is therefore with some relief that I step aside from this duty today and leave it in the capable hands of Charlie and my husband.

Radar, to his credit, takes the whole visit in his stride and seems to treat it as yet another opportunity to be fondled lovingly by his adoring public and be the centre of attention. Even if this means one of his fan club casually sticks a needle in his scruff.

So far so good, but upon their return, they recount that according to the vet, we have made a major life mistake.

Admittedly, there have been fleeting moments when I would have wholeheartedly agreed with him, but overall, he's a good dog and this seems very out of character coming from the normally calm and positive demeanour of the vet.

What on earth could have happened?

I probe further and discover that it wasn't the decision to get a dog *per se* that was being maligned by the vet, but rather the fact that we chose a male dog over a bitch. Apparently, the girls are much easier to manage, albeit rather dull, whilst boys offer challenge but are far more interesting. I am unsure as to how interesting and exciting I need my life to be at this point and am pretty sure that I could think of better ways to get a buzz than manage the mischief of a male dog. I wonder if his comments were in any way linked to cake-gate?

Still, overall, other than also being told to avoid over-feeding him as he was looking just a tiny bit chunky around the thighs (Really? I'm almost coming out in sympathy with Radar on this point and am doubly glad now that I wasn't accompanying him), he received a clean bill of health.

Thursday 16th March

We have made some very small steps in progressing with Project-Squeaky-Toy on Radar's walks and have purchased two new ones for this very purpose. One is designed to resemble a cheese sandwich, albeit a rather rubbery one, and the other takes the shape of a large sausage.

Perhaps on reflection it might have been wiser to have picked something smaller in the sausage department – whilst its size makes it easy to grasp and is proving very appealing to the dog, there is always the risk that it might not fit fully into your pocket and that you will be faced with having to explain why carrying around such a large length of rubber is integral to your dog training regime. But let's not overthink this. The point is, that so far, the distraction has worked perfectly.

A short distance from the danger point at the brow of the hill on the return leg of the walk, I attach the lead to ensure maximum control; then, at the merest hint of a leap, I squeeze the sausage...and would you believe it...Radar stops short and finds himself forgetting all about his monster moment in lieu of thoughts of a giant squeaky meat feast!

Who would have thought?

Obviously, to avoid him becoming too accustomed to the sausage, I will have to alternate with the squeaky sandwich which has a slightly different pitch to it, and perhaps the rhythm of the squeaks could also be experimented with, but overall, I sense we might be onto something big.

Friday 17th March

I really must take more care over what I think. No sooner have I mused over the potential complications of explaining sausage scenarios, and the universe runs with it, having a good laugh at my expense.

In this case, I wasn't within 10 miles of the dog, nor was I out for a walk. I had simply taken some time out to buy a section of ceramic tap and a new plug chain from the DIY store. The plug chain was in fact an impulse purchase in a moment of unadulterated plumbing enthusiasm, but that is by the by. The point of this is that just as I was packing the shiny new chain into my handbag, it slipped from my hand onto the shop floor. Bending down to pick it up, I unexpectedly let out a loud and prolonged squeaking sound, which rest assured had nothing to do with my own plumbing, and everything to do with the squeaky rubber sandwich still lurking in my pocket. I tried to explain the situation to the shop assistant, producing the sandwich as evidence. She seemed to struggle to hide her amusement but I can't be sure if this was down to my embarrassed explanation or the antics of my dog. By this point a long queue was beginning to form behind me and I felt it best to make a swift exit.

Saturday 18th March

Finally, the day has come. This-afternoon Operation Dog Psychologist is officially underway.

Feeling a mix of nervous anticipation and guarded optimism about how this might pan out, we gather *en famille* and await the arrival of Olivia who has been assigned to our case. Radar has now behaved impeccably for three weeks which is as encouraging as it is disconcerting.

Will he give Olivia any indication of his alter ego?

Can we really believe in the head psychologist's assurances that Radar's issues are quite normal and could be resolved in a single session?

Who knows? But at this point, I am perfectly happy to run with this utopian vision of a miracle cure.

Olivia arrives promptly, rings the doorbell as is greeted by Radar's best wag, charming smile and a well-loved blanket. He is the picture of endearing and I suspect that despite his questionable resumé, she is already smitten and is putting all our troubles down to inexperienced dog-parenting rather than a defect with this amiable melty, brown-eyed dog. She has of course come well-armed, producing, as she joins us on the sofa, a sack load of liver cake morsels.

Radar melts and they are putty in each other's paws.

We, however, are not feeling quite so confident. Or at least I'm not. Doug begins to explain how Radar never jumps at him and how successful he has been with the dog-training. I on the other hand, recount a catalogue a dog-related trauma that must seem hard to believe. To her credit, she listens diplomatically to these to contradictory tales, nodding understandingly and making it all seem totally normal. I find myself pondering if this is what marriage guidance feels like and wonder if she offers this as a side-line, but my thoughts are interrupted.

"Perhaps we could take him out for his normal walk as see him at his worse?" Olivia light-heartedly suggests, making it very clear that I am to be her partner on this mission.

"What an excellent Idea!" I reply, in a pathetic attempt to feign genuine enthusiasm.

Not that I don't want to face this head on. Of course I do. But I have serious doubts about whether that pocketful of liver cake is going to entice him to make an enemy of himself in any shape or form.

And then there is her hoodie

Emblazoned across her back for all to see, is a marvellous bit of company advertising, which to all intents and purposes might as well have read:

' HERE TO TRAIN CLUELESS OWNERS

AND

THEIR *TERRIBLY* BEHAVED DOGS'

Not that I was feeling in the least self-conscious about the situation.

How could I be?

I am a fully grown adult and therefore totally ~~flawed~~ capable of womanning-up to this scenario.

We walk without incident to the danger point at the top of the hill and try to entice Radar to expose his naughtier underbelly by turning on our heels and heading home.

Nothing.

Not a hint of misbehaviour.

Olivia suggests we repeat this routine a few times to give him the chance to perform, but the closest he comes is a gentle leap towards her pocket as he catches a particularly pungent waft of liver cake, before promptly remembering his manners and adopting a half-sit until the treat has been suitably administered.

Could it be that he has been cured by liver cake alone? Could I have funded a lifetime's supply at less than the cost of Olivia's fee? I push these musings to the back of my mind.

Olivia, however, has a different view on the situation. She suggests that this repeated toing and froing at the top of the hill might be part of the solution and that every time Radar shows the slightest hint of bad behaviour on the return leg, we should turn around and extend the walk.

Clearly, I am in no position to argue, but I silently wonder if this is like giving a toddler a trip to the sweet shop every time they throw a strop? It also makes me think of a nursery rhyme about marching up and down hills endlessly, but I expect that this is another rather ineffective default setting by my brain to self-soothe. It's not working.

I say nothing.

My mind, however, is in overdrive. Am I to be eternally subjected to walks with no fixed end point, accompanied by a dog who only has to glare at me to get a few more minutes out in the field? Did I do something outrageous in a previous life to deserve this?

Preoccupied with this uncomfortable train of thought, I only half hear Olivia's additional suggestion that equipping myself with a water bottle to squirt when in imminent danger, can work wonders for bringing errant dogs into line.

Returning home, we all reconvene for Olivia to summarise her findings to the whole family. To their credit, Doug and kids all listen politely and seem genuinely impressed by the logical and straightforward suggestions she has put in place. We thank her profusely as she reassures us that Radar is perfectly manageable, and this behaviour is very common in young dogs. As I close the door behind her, I return to sit down with some sense of relief. I *really* want to believe her.

"Well, that wasn't what I expected" announces Sascha.

"No, that was really weird" agrees Charlie.

Assuming they are precociously understanding the implications of spoiling the dog in the manner suggested by extending his walks, I am on the verge of commending their insight into rearing the young when Sascha stops me in my tracks.

"What happened to all the whispering?" she asks.

Doug and I stare at each other across the room, completely perplexed.

"Yeah, I thought she was just going to whisper in his ear to get him to stop all that jumping" declares Charlie, clearly quite put out by the relatively normal turn of the afternoon's events.

Turns out, that the kids were expecting some sort of hypnotic magic show to be performed in their living room, involving mystical sweet-nothings being gently whispered into Radar's ear thereby invoking a miracle cure, rather than a straightforward walk and the suggestion of an extreme exercise regime. This of course was entirely the fault of their parents, who had casually been referring to the dog psychologist as a 'Dog Whisperer' for the last few weeks.

Quite how two intelligent teenagers could genuinely believe this, took us somewhat by surprise, but, apparently we are living in an era of fake news which I guess can blur the wobbly line between fantasy and common sense.

But really? For F***'s Sake!

Sunday 19th March

Top secret operation 'Grand Old Duke of York' is officially underway. Of course, not a word of this has been whispered to the dog as that might give the game away, and so it is that I head out for our walk with a spring in my step and an unflappable confidence that I *absolutely* have the upper paw.

Such are my high spirits, that as we march up the hill, I even find myself cheerfully adapting the lyrics of that catchy pre-school hit to suit my mood.

Oh, the Grand Old Hill we climb

We'll make ten thousand steps

We only have to do this march

Until Radar 's tired out!

And when we are up we are up

And when we'll go down dog knows,

And when we are only halfway up

Our direction no one knows!

Yay!....and repeat!

Again

And again...

Apologies to anybody listening to this as an audiobook, but an out of tune rendition is essential for the purposes of a realistic account. Traditional readers will just have to use their imaginations or test it out for themselves perhaps.

Anyway, back to the march.

Everything was going well until I decided to think about making our first descent towards home. At this point, my mind-reading dog realised that this was his moment to step into action and allow me to fully employ operation GODOY, hereafter to be known as operation YOYO DOG in a cunning reversal of the letters with a sneaky extra YO in recognition of the endless ups and downs – not a chance he'll crack that one. Ha! Cunning as a fox I am!

Turns out that Radar has a hint more fox about him than I do.

Perhaps it was the subtle change in rhythm of my pace, or a momentary repositioning of the lead in preparation for our downward trek, but before I had a chance to call him to heel, he darted around me with a flurry of agile leaps and bounds and a full set of four upper paws.

Yes. I know that that defies the laws of gravity. But I'm quite sure this is how it was.

This of course, would have been the perfect moment to pull out the squirty water bottle and bring him back to his senses. Had I remembered to pack the squirty water bottle. But in my enthusiasm for the march and focussed entirely on that flawless YOYO DOG plan, I'd forgotten to bring it with me. Damn it.

There was nothing for it but to turn back up the hill and hope that this would confuse Radar's game plan. There was also nothing pleasurable about being hounded up the hill by a leaping dog, intent on testing the limits of my determination to follow through. To be fair, he was playing his part impeccably – to get through this he had to genuinely tire of his game and resign himself to me no longer being easy prey, but in that moment, I was a long way from seeing things in this light. This was feeling like another abysmal failure.

We repeated YOYO DOG a few more times, and whilst the renditions of my marching mantra became noticeably less jolly as they were forced through gritted teeth, Radar was clearly showing early signs of confusion. The severity of his leaps was diminishing ever so slightly and as he glanced at me with signs of hope that we might be forever on the point of extending his walk, I sensed that we might just be onto something.

This, for now, was enough to get us home without further incident. I'm pretty sure that in future, armed with the water bottle, I will be invincible.

Friday 24th March

This week we have employed a new walking strategy:

- Do not leave the house without the water bottle.
- Show the bottle to the dog at the beginning of the walk and at the slightest hint of bad behaviour.
- Put the dog on the lead well before the danger point and before turning for home.
- Employ Operation YOYO DOG repeatedly.
- Carry a backup squeaky plastic sandwich / giant sausage.

I am delighted to report, that so far this week daily test marches have been incident free. There was only one point when he needed to be shown the water bottle, at which point, he thought twice and resumed doe-eyed Labrador status.

Saturday 25th March

Two weeks ago, we lost Radar's head collar. This was something we had been testing to give us a little more control when he's walking on the lead. Radar, however, decided that it needed to be put through a more challenging evaluation process and so performed an impressive Houdini-style escape, skilfully freeing himself from what he concluded was a seriously flawed piece of kit. How he did this and where he hid it was a mystery to us, but today he must have had a change of heart. During one of his 'very important' sniff stops, he suddenly became particularly enthusiastic about checking out the depths of an otherwise non-descript patch of undergrowth, to emerge seconds later with the head collar and a beaming grin between his teeth. Having completely forgotten his distaste for the collar, he was almost as excited as me as I showered him with praise. So much so in fact, that not five minutes later, he dived into another bush and came out clutching another dog's lead. To clarify, there was no other free-rein dog or owner in sight so we can safely assume that rather than having chosen to embark on some sort of canine freedom mission après Amnesty International, he was probably just out to be rewarded with an extra treat.

Mothering Sunday 26th March

My reward for being a mother today was really quite remarkable. Not only was I treated to a walk with my son and the dog under glorious blue skies and spring sunshine, but in a bizarre turn of events, Charlie didn't complain about the very moderate distance, nor did he insist on employing his diverse range of questionable and regressive dog-training techniques that seem designed solely to sate his own need for power and entertainment. In cahoots with Charlie, Radar deigned to behave like a well-trained and adorable Labrador, abstaining from all delinquent behaviour. I am fully aware that this state of affairs won't last beyond today but for now I am wallowing happily in this moment like a dog in fox poo.

Tuesday 29th March

Poo sticks versus Pooh sticks:

Radar and I have been watching the news together this week and have noticed that the debate over whether to bag his poo or flick it with a stick into a nearby hedge, has raised its head again. Together, we have discussed this at length, and I have pointed out that I am not prepared for either of us to carry a long stick with us on walks for this purpose. The thought of gripping the wrong end in a moment of confusion, or worse, him deciding to play fetch with said stick and confuse the issue further, is a hard line for me. And, to be honest, hunting through the undergrowth at the required moment in the hope of coming across a suitable stick for this purpose is also a definite no. Before we know it, the hedgerows along popular walking routes might be full of pre-used sticks to fool the casual hunter, not to mention the potential for branches to be splattered from previous flicks. Sorry, I may well be over thinking this but for now I'm resigned to sticking with pockets full of poo bags.

Radar participates in these discussions with a thoughtful and quizzical silence, which may be interpreted to the uninitiated as indifference. I can assure you however, that it is not. Today I witnessed absolute proof of his genius in problem solving on this matter, when he insisted, despite being still on the lead, on showing me the way forward. This involved dragging both of us into the hedge, him doing his business well off the path but in the most inaccessible and prickly part of the hedge that he could access, before extricating us both to proceed with his walk free of stick and plastic. He is proving himself to be a true eco warrior, although I'm the only one bearing the war wounds to prove it with a well snagged t-shirt and a set of bramble scratches up my arms. Maybe next time he can do it off the lead.

In fact, maybe next time we'll take a walk by the river instead and I can demonstrate what the game Pooh sticks was really intended for.

Saturday 1st April

Another morning of dog training with Shuna and it did not go exactly to plan.

Firstly, I was gently reprimanded for turning up alone. Not that I'd forgotten to bring the dog - I'm not that absent minded. I had however neglected to drag my husband out of bed and bring him along for an hour of fun and frolics in the field. Shuna politely asked if I might be able to pop back and get him in a tone of voice that left me and Radar realising that saying he was still in bed enjoying a lie-in just wouldn't cut it. There is no denying that dog training is so much more than being just for the dog.

Fifteen minutes later, decidedly bleary eyed and still a little stiff, Doug had joined us in the field and was paired up with Radar for the warm-up exercise, working towards developing Radar's self-control in the face of temptation. This is not a strong point for him, and to be fair, I totally get that – put me in front of a plate of gooey chocolate brownies and they really don't stand a chance. Not that there was a single brownie on offer to sweeten the morning's activities, that would have to wait, but instead, the 'treat' that Radar had to resist was me.

Under different circumstances I might have taken this as a compliment, but it soon became apparent that from my point of view, this was going to be a lose-lose scenario - if Radar couldn't resist running towards me, then he'd fail in his task, and if he could, I'm left to contemplate my allure even in the eyes of my generally adoring dog.

As Radar and Doug stood in the centre of the field, I was instructed to head to the far side with Shuna's perfectly behaved terrier, Bill. No doubt this was intended to enhance my appeal, in case he should feel torn between his delectable mistress and a quick frolic with a fellow dog. Still, I like to think of myself as fairly broad-shouldered and so stood my ground with Bill and awaited our fate. Remarkably, Radar was, so far, behaving well, and trotting at Doug's heels with little interest in my supposedly irresistible presence across the field. It was only when Shuna played her trump card and began to head across to join Bill and me that Radar's resistance to temptation was pushed over the edge.

Such was his determination not to be left out of the action, that he unexpectedly changed course, tugging Doug over into the mud, escaping his grasp and bounding over to join the party on the far side.

Doug has now spent the rest of the day even more uncomfortable than when he woke up and worried that he might have caused himself more damage. Radar, having by this point consumed a large number of training treats has shown no remorse and is not only hyperactive, but then proceeded to have a bout of diarrhoea.

Perhaps sensing that we needed a little extra support, I opened my inbox this-evening to discover that Shuna has filled it with a vast and comprehensive selection of dog-training articles. Her level of dedication to Radar's welfare is phenomenal, though I now feel obliged to do her justice and read, study and act upon them before our next session. This feels almost as intense as studying for a master's degree in dog behaviour.

Surely the rest of the dog owning population can't be going through this?

What exactly are we doing wrong?

Do we have a particularly challenging dog? Or worse, are we failing as dog-parents?

Sunday 2nd April

As with so much in life, there are often different ways of looking at the same scenario. This morning was a case in point.

The upbeat version of this morning's walk plays

out like this:

A beautiful day of blue skies and spring sunshine beckoned. Charlie agrees to accompany me on our walk even though it drags him away from his computer and the important task of developing his career as a future YouTube billionaire.

We stop to chat to a neighbour and enjoy a few moments enjoying their spectacular display of tulips as Radar sits patiently at our sides. After a few minutes we head to the fields, well equipped with a ball thrower to give Radar some extra fun and exercise before heading back towards the ford for cooling paddle, where we bump into an adorable young puppy and his owner. Even as we are forced to stop and move aside for a couple of cars and a small terrier to pass, Radar maintains excellent behaviour and self-control, offering the other dog a short sniff of the backside as he passes through. Heading back we wave to one of Radar's favourite people - Shuna's husband John, as he passes in his truck.

On the other hand, it could be described slightly differently:

The shopping delivery is due in 1 hour. This leaves just enough time to get Radar out for a decent walk. Except that I am determined that Charlie should come too get some sort of screen break. Reluctantly (and that's good enough for me), he accepts, although it takes him an inordinate length of time to get ready to leave the house as he suddenly declares that he has no trousers that fit as he is growing faster than I can shop. We eventually find an acceptable pair on the floor and make it to the pavement where we see our neighbours and so stop for a chat about her impressive tulip display (mine were eaten by squirrels but let's not dwell on that) and how she had been to Crufts this year where she was overcome with the array of happy, waggy and obedient dogs she met and how remarkably well-trained they all were. She then turns with a smile towards Radar and asks me how we are getting on with him.

Whilst considering the possibility of responding with an unequivocal and socially acceptable 'great', as opposed to the more honest 'a work in progress', qualified by an explanation of the weight of responsibility versus the delights of having such a lovely companion, we are joined by another close neighbour. I suspect that they probably very quickly wish that they had simply walked on by rather than join our chat as the conversation takes an unfortunate turn into darker territory. Inexplicably, Charlie and I are soon enduring a sad description of the day our cat died after getting hit by a car in this very spot and the haunting nature of subsequent sounds of his grave being dug as they echoed across the neighbourhood.

As swiftly and politely as humanly possibly I decided that there was now an urgent need to extricate ourselves from the conversation and let Radar have his walk.

This went fairly smoothly, except that 'smoothly' when walking with Charlie, is rarely stress free. On this occasion he was equipped with a tennis ball thrower and an air of confidence in the quality of his aim that I didn't share as it repeatedly whistled past my ear at a hair's breadth and into the far reaches of the adjoining field. Radar however, loved this game and leapt at the chance to run and find the ball or sniff it out, but never actually retrieve it. Despite clear instructions to aim the ball away from the crops and not to trample them, Charlie raced to rescue the abandoned ball completely deaf to my protestations. By this point all thoughts of blue skies and the joy of the great outdoors were evaporating rapidly. And this was not the end of it. Alongside the ball thrower, Charlie was also equipped with a camera attached to a selfie stick which he was waving around as if he was about to throw it for the dog once we'd lost all alternative projectiles. At least, this is how Radar was seeing the situation. Second by second the dog began to lose more and more control as the two of them leapt around me as I hopelessly attempted to bring an air of calm to the situation. It goes without saying that the camera was filming every second of this charade and the camera angles were far from complimentary.

To cool everyone off, we wandered home via the ford for a paddle and a dip which would have been fine if it hadn't been for Charlie running ahead to greet a lady walking with a new puppy. Finding himself unable to bear being left behind, Radar pulls me precariously and at speed towards the pool party with cars travelling in both directions at the narrowest point along the verge. Fiercely gripping the lead and demanding he stops and sits proves exceptionally challenging as I desperately try to remember the training tactics for ensuring he can resist temptation. Unfortunately, all I can recall is Doug falling flat on his face into the mud. It is at this point that one of the drivers waves at me and I see that it is one of Radar's favourite people -Shuna's husband John, who fully witnesses our chaotic demise and will no doubt enjoying recounting it back home over a cup of tea. I double my efforts to appear in control and we all make it across the ford intact.

On a positive note, I was by this point so well-primed for all eventualities, that when we pass two frighteningly fierce and snarling Staffordshire Bull Terriers on our way home, I was able to steer us past them under complete control and not get eaten alive.

Wednesday 5th April

Thought of the Day:

Very often, I feel as though I'm running around, chasing my tail. It struck me this evening that my dog does this for fun. I have no idea what the moral to this tale (tail?) is, but I'm pretty sure Radar has got it more sussed than me.

Saturday 15th April

Yet another spontaneous but exciting purchase from the garden centre dog emporium - a poo bag dispenser.

I totally get that this may not initially sound like an obvious source of excitement, but sometimes you just have to grab a bit of joy where you can find it and here it is - a palm-sized solution to the bottomless pit of bags stuffed in every pocket. No longer will they be blown across the countryside as they fall from my pocket whenever I dive in for a treat or a tissue, nor will I risk running out at an inopportune moment, with the capacity to carry a roll of fifty with me at any time.

I go home smug with delight about my new purchase anticipating with a cosy glow the ease with which I will dispense poo bags from now on.

Only, it turns out that there is a slight snag with these bag dispensers. Radar was as enthusiastic to test it as I was and, in the process, we have both discovered that such is its usability in the dispensing department, that dogs are just as capable of unravelling a bag or two as their owners. Or to be precise, dogs can unravel all fifty at once. Should one try to reverse this process, by grabbing at the trail of bags, you might find that your dog proves himself to be perfectly capable of separating them, thoughtfully saving you the trouble of tearing them off yourself. You will then have a large supply of loose bags which may now be *ever so slightly* torn. Not sufficiently to be easily spotted, but more than enough to ensure a kind of Russian roulette experience in terms of leakage, should you dare to use one of these bags in the future.

It is really great having a dog to test ~~you~~ things to the max like this.

Sunday 16th April

Radar appeared a little on edge today and has been exhibiting a range of odd phobias. Admittedly, he may have been feeling a little camera shy as his paparazzi, in the form of Charlie, joined us again this-afternoon with the mission of capturing a range of odd close-ups that will probably be viewed as highly artistic in a couple of hundred years.

It seems though that Radar was struggling with seeing things from odd and jaunty angles and has spent his walk warning us of the terrible danger we are about to expose ourselves to in the face of the following items:

A bouquet of pheasants*

Two teenage girls sitting in the grass (clearly he was wondering where their legs were and why they were so short)

A wheelbarrow casually abandoned in the middle of the path.

Two open umbrellas left on my neighbour's doorstep to dry.

Each and every one of these perils was bravely growled at from a distance, and, with hackles protectively raised whilst clinging to my side, we skirted each impostor with heroic courage.

*I have just googled the collective noun for a group of pheasants and what a selection there was to behold - it was almost as complex as choosing from the fifty Eskimo words for snow. For those as excited as me about this discovery, the options included a covey, a nide, a nye, an eye and a brace (although the latter wasn't quite the gathering I was aiming for as these ones were very much alive). Bouquet however was for me the clear winner – it seems this conjuring up images of the pheasants flying out of the undergrowth and reaching for the skies in a flash of colourful feathers. This is exactly what happened when Radar ventured to a little close to their bush.

Monday 24th April

Not only was this the first day back at work after the Easter holiday, but for some reason it had seemed like a good idea to cap this off with a late afternoon training session with Shuna in a nearby field.

What this really amounted to, was a session of ego-boosting for Doug, who despite not having read any of Shuna's training tips and emails, gets the dog to perform perfectly. For me however, it was more like an hour of ritual humiliation. The 'tricks' that Radar and Doug can perform with a magical and slick flick of the wrist continue to completely elude me as I repeatedly try to bring him to heel and turn us smoothly in a harmonious waltz of woman and dog.

This does not happen with any degree of elegance or coordination. The angle we end up in is not right. Under pressure, I turn in the wrong direction and then Radar follows making us doubly in the wrong. I feel like I am right back in my ballet class, age five, which required levels of balance and poise that were so lacking that I barely made it beyond the first term.

"Try to look a little more enticing" Shuna suggests from the far side of the field "You need to distract him from licking the cowpat!"

Enticing? FFS! How exactly? And am I really so

much less appealing than the cowpat in question?

Most days, I barely manage to make myself look enticing to myself, let alone any human admirers, but now I've got to do it for the dog?

Should I be adjusting my make-up to give me more canine appeal? Or fishing tennis balls out of every orifice and juggling them in a teasing manner? Maybe I need to get down on all fours and roll on my back?

Needless to say, I am far too polite to voice these thoughts out loud and in spite of my dismal failure to coordinate and entice my dog, I can see that I have provided some top-quality entertainment to my audience. And Radar got a lot of pleasure from licking that cowpat, so I'd say the training session was quite a success.

Sunday 30th April

I am alone with Radar overnight. The rest of the family have gone away to visit family in Wales leaving Radar and I to some quality time together. He however seems somewhat sceptical about the 'quality' of what might be on offer and has been sulking since they left yesterday morning. This seems a harsh reminder of how I need to make myself more alluring to him and so I have given the matter some considerable time and thought and I can confidently declare that I have had a revelation.

The solution lies not in my exterior appearance, but of course, entirely upon what lies on the inside. The inside that is, of my pockets. There is nothing that keeps him at my side more reliably than a few extra lumps and bumps around the hips as I ensure that an ample supply of meaty treats are stuffed into every crevice.

On the upside, the immediate implementation of this strategy, meant that we managed to successfully navigate the afternoon's walk with both of us ignoring every passing fellow dog walker. To play my part properly this meant spotting the oncoming threat well in advance, turning away from them and focussing entirely on Radar repeatedly feeding him treats and reminding him what a good boy he was until the danger had passed. The only problem with this was that it all felt rather rude. I couldn't even explain myself for fear of taking my eye off the game and Radar grasping the opportunity to leap in their direction. We were however rewarded for our endeavours by one passer-by commenting on how obedient my dog was.

Ha! If only they knew!

What my dog is, is *very* greedy.

Sunday 21st May

Living with Radar often feels like taking a joyride along the trajectory of one of those A&E heartrate monitors where it's a constant flow of ups and downs and then, every now and again, an ominously smooth flat line. Well, today was a case in point. The last two weeks have been breathtakingly and uncannily smooth, lulling us into a delicate sense of security, and so it should have been hardly surprising to be jolted right back to reality with a bang this-morning.

But frustratingly, it took the form of another punch in the stomach.

In this case, the unfortunate turn of events centred around the delivery of a parcel at the very moment we headed out for a walk. To save the driver the trouble of knocking at the door to find nobody in, I thought it might be helpful to wait for her to get the package from her van before heading off on our walk. However, this unplanned pause proved far too much for Radar who became increasingly excited about the prospect of someone to say hello to and by the time she emerged from the back of her van, he was pulling frantically, bouncing madly and refusing to sit still while I signed for the package. Radar of course was way ahead of his time – us mere humans had no idea that in some not so distant future, no one would care about signing for stuff anymore and instead we would be greeting delivery drivers as if they were the only people we'd seen for days, but he had no way to tell us this.

Instead, the delivery lady offered to hold him while I signed and the next thing I know she is on her knees in front of me trying to stop her wrist getting twisted up in the lead. I am completely mortified and feel awful despite her protestations that she is *absolutely fine*. She might have felt differently if by this point she had noticed the amount of muck and mud all over her jeans, but I can't bring myself to point this out and wish her a sheepish goodbye.

Ironically, the package contained a pair of new jeans. Let's just hope they fit or I might have to relive this whole thing again.

Monday 29th May

Doug has been working on a new hobby. He has had many of these over the years that have ranged from model railways and astronomy to flight simulation, but this one is of particular interest as it involves turning the kitchen table and back room (currently the domain of the dog) into a production line for bassoon reeds to provide himself and Sascha with an endless supply. Whilst this seems like a practical hobby to fit in with his new more sedentary life, Radar and I have a few concerns over the potential for our domestic space to be completely and indefinitely overrun with reeds, cotton and shavings. I have discussed this with Radar on one of our walks and asked him for his opinion and for advice on how we should broach this issue with Doug. Radar assured me through his deep and silent, brown-eyed stare that he would give this some thought and get back to me with a few suggestions.

I didn't have to wait long.

It turns out that a small length of casually cast aside reed has almost the same chewability and allure to a Labrador as a morsel of stick or bone. No doubt he had been influenced by watching his master place them in his mouth and emitting an intriguing squeaky whistle sound, but Radar's thoughtful testing regime of grabbing them at every opportunity and depositing the best ones in a frayed pile in the garden was a clear declaration that this project needed to be moved elsewhere.

I think Radar would make an excellent marriage guidance counsellor.

Sunday 4th June

Radar's prowess as a marriage guidance counsellor is in direct opposition to his potential as a guard dog.

This-morning, I was quietly taking a moment

to pluck my eyebrows, taking advantage of the sunlight beaming through my bedroom window, when out of the corner of my eye I see a man walk across the drive, straight past the front door, and march, bold as brass, through the side gate into the back garden. I hear him call out a couple of times, but not loud enough to hear what he is saying and then he doesn't seem to reappear. Where on earth is he? I creep downstairs keeping an eye of the front windows to see if I can spot his departure, whilst moving as swiftly and silently as possible to lock the rear doors whilst Radar sleeps peacefully, oblivious to the potential intruder.

Still no sign of anyone. Part of me remains on high alert and ready to arm myself with a heavy iron frying pan, and the other part is busy rationalising this as a meter-reader or perhaps someone attempting to retrieve a wandering lost dog.

And then I have a brainwave. We have recently installed one of those Ring doorbells that record movement and on checking through the footage, I can clearly see someone walking in …but there is no sign of them coming out.

By this point, Radar has just about managed to open an eye onto the proceedings, perhaps sniffing the sense of rising fear in the air and I decide this might the moment to encourage him to get up and do some proper guard duty. As I kneel down to stir him further, I spot a parcel just beside the door mat that definitely wasn't there earlier.

Everything falls into place. The 'intruder' was another parcel delivery, by someone who clearly didn't spot the front door. I guess they realised their mistake as they found themselves in the back garden faced with an open back door and a large but lazy guard dog, and dropped the delivery and beat a retreat so quickly that neither the doorbell or the sleeping dog could catch them.

I suppose I should at least be grateful that we don't have a dog vicious enough to have torn the intruder to shreds, although I think there might be room for improvement in suggesting that he at least pretends to sound scary when strangers leave presents for us. Maybe I can bring this up in the next dog-training session?

Monday 5th June

Radar has taken my advice about sounding scary to heart. Today he growled and threatened to chase a black cat up a tree as it glared at him from across the street on our evening walk. He also barked and raised his hackles at a skateboard that was daring to sit stubbornly abandoned and unmoved by his warnings in the back garden. I am feeling encouraged.

Thursday 8th June – General Election Day

Well, I managed to make it up to the village hall

this-evening to cast my vote in today's national lottery. It appears though I had failed to engage in the most important job on General Election day for a dog owner – allowing Radar to star in the latest social media trend: #Dogs at polling stations.

If only I had been possessed of a little more foresight, I could have planned a statement outfit for him that would have clearly expressed his stance on Brexit, the increasingly precarious Tory majority and the 'juicy bone' of free university tuition fees thrown into the mix by the opposition. Or I could have just videoed him marking his territory on the voting booths or rolling on his back to have his tummy tickled by the candidate with the deepest pockets stuffed with the tastiest titbits, but I'm afraid I failed abysmally on all fronts.

I will plan better next time round.

Saturday 10th June

Oh, the joys of Summer! As thanks for a glorious and long afternoon walk through fields and meadows of gently swaying grasses, Radar let loose an enormous grass pollen induced sneeze and immediately wiped an explosion of snot all over my trousers. Nice.

This may seem to be a simple sneeze brought along by a high pollen count, but such is Radar's subtly of expression and ability to get to the heart of issues of personal and national importance, that I think we can confidently assume that he is actually making an important political statement, having missed his opportunity yesterday.

Our newly re-elected Prime Minister, Theresa May has been reported as having partaken in some quite outrageous activity in the field when questioned on the matter of the naughtiest thing that she has ever done. Apparently, as a child her rebellion peaked at the moment that she decided to run, carefree, through a farmer's crops, much to his fury. Personally, I can't see what he was complaining about - at least he didn't get covered in snot as she emerged from the waves of wheat.

Secretly, I am quite proud that Radar isn't the only one exhibiting inappropriate behaviour in the fields and meadows of rural England and that my dog has surpassed even a major world leader in his capacity to show such daring and rebellious behaviour on a daily basis. But perhaps he needs to temper his competitive edge - next thing we know, Radar and his fellow hounds will be implying that leaders will be brought to their knees and hung out to dry for sipping wine in the Downing Steet garden and sneezing on the rest of the nation as we try not to catch a nasty virus. Highly improbable. Really must stop reading too much into his behaviour. He is only a dog after all.

Friday 16th June

An unusual turn of events as I stopped at Aldi to grab a few bits for the weekend on the way home today to find that the entrance was being guarded by a friendly but clearly unaccompanied chocolate Labrador. He appeared to be waiting for someone to let him follow them in and perhaps offer assistance to reach any top shelf sausages that he might fancy saving from the BBQ at the weekend. But, bad luck for him, he got us. Sascha immediately leapt into dog rescue mode, even though I suspect he had no desire to be repatriated, as she duly checked his collar for contact details.

Bingo! A mobile number led to a quick ring home and the grateful but embarrassed explanation that although he was a bit of a Houdini, a trip to the supermarket was a first even for him.

Owner and dog were promptly reunited and let's hope that there was no more to it. Surely training your dog to queue for you and pick up provisions at a supermarket would only be useful in the event of some sort of zombie apocalypse?

Saturday 15th July

As the school year draws to a close and weeks of holiday beckon, I feel strangely lulled into an almost comfortable sense of security. We have had almost a month of delightful and refreshingly unremarkable days with Radar. There has been no jumping, he has shown a vague capacity to walk on the lead at heel, and he even remembered to come when called on occasion.

No, you know what? It's way more than a sense of security – I'm actually verging on jubilant with an overdose of smugness.

Because today I feel like I've graduated. Not perhaps in the sense of a first-class honours from Oxbridge in Pedigree Pup Endurance, but perhaps a decent pass at GCSE. And to be honest, that's good enough and I'm quite proud. I realise that this is a dangerous thing to claim, and it will no doubt come back and bite me, but for now, let's run with it.

This all came about when I picked up Radar from his mini-break with Shuna this-afternoon, to be told that that he has shown a remarkable improvement in his behaviour with other dogs. For the first time he was willing to accept that they didn't always want to play with him and was able to move on as well as be a gentle and exemplary playmate to some of the younger dogs.

And then there was the evening walk. Now, I know that this can often be the precursor to a more negative twist in the tale of the dog, but this was not one of them. As we strolled through the village, Radar was on his best behaviour, exhibiting world class lead walking and treat taking, when we bumped into a couple who had been unfortunate enough to witness his less controlled ramblings on a regular basis.

'Well, how long has it taken to get him to that point?' they ask in a tone of awe and muted surprise.

I hold back from suggesting that three days at the dog sitter's chasing a hyperactive spaniel might have had something to do with his calmer demeanour, and instead decide to ride the crest of this rare wave of glory.

'It's been 18 months of really challenging ups and downs to be sure, but I think we're finally getting there' I reply with a genuine glimmer of conviction.

A look of shock flashes fleetingly across their faces as they glance down at their feet, and I realise that they are exactly where we were a year or so ago. There, with a mischievous glint in its eye, wriggles a small and sprightly labradoodle. They adopted him a week ago after he was returned to the breeder for being too much of a handful for the first owners. I offer some reassuring platitudes and wish them well and as we head off in the opposite direction, I whisper 'good boy' to Radar to thank him for his service to new dog owners in pretending that he has grown into the perfect dog. We wander home and I am unable to stifle a self-satisfied grin. My acting career is clearly taking off.

Saturday 22nd July

 WE HAVE A PRIZE-WINNING DOG!

OK – I know that's a massive spoiler, but this has to be one of the proudest moments that Radar and I have ever experienced and was achieved through brutal perseverance and borderline insanity.

For a number of weeks, the village notice boards and local magazine have been advertising the annual village fun day and dog show. This did not seem like an event that Radar and I would be ideally suited to - hundreds of people, hordes of high-achieving dogs and plenty of small children and tasty treats, did not tempt me to test him in this way.

Radar had been a little less definitive in this regard and had shown a passing interest in the posters by weeing on the posts they were attached to and occasional sniffing and studying one hung at a nose level on some railings.

And yet somehow, we found ourselves turning up.

I have no idea why.

For a start, it was pouring with rain, and to add to the challenging conditions, only Charlie and I were home today, so we would be completely alone managing Radar's uncontrollable levels of exuberance that he saves especially for exciting and new situations. Visualising him trotting obediently to heel or calmly exhibiting his pedigree credentials to an audience was frankly unimaginable.

We were not wrong.

Queuing for the entry tickets to our chosen classes was challenge enough. Radar didn't approve of waiting in line and felt that the only activity worth pursuing was to sniff and play with all the other dogs in the queue or attempt to barge his way to the front. Despite our best attempts at control, even the treats we offered to incite his cooperation were insufficient to tempt him away from such an array of beauties, and both fellow owners and their dogs were becoming snootily disenchanted with his 'friendly' approaches and disregard for the rules of maintaining a polite tail's wag between them.

What to do? Leave Charlie with an over-excited dog and grab the tickets and quickly as possible, whilst risking him being pulled at speed into the nearest hot dog stand? Or leave Charlie to take control of the booking of the classes and see what we ended up with?

Being still in possession of a couple of responsible bones in my body, I grabbed the dog and left Charlie in charge of Radar's fate. Either way, challenges lay ahead - first up in the afternoon's schedule were the pedigree classes, but the thought of getting this over and done with quickly were completely outweighed by the sheer humiliation potential in attempting to strut our stuff alongside a pack of such seasoned professionals. On the other hand, waiting in the pouring rain for 2 hours to compete in the more light-hearted categories with a hyperactive hound by my side wasn't sounding that great either.

"Mum!" shouted Charlie as he raced across the arena with a handful of tickets. "We're entered for 'Best Looking Dog' and 'Dog with the Waggiest Tail'!"

I am quite touched by this – it wasn't that long ago that Charlie thought we had made the worst decision of our lives by getting a dog, and I like to think that maybe this shows he's developed at least a sneaking admiration for our charming but high-spirited chum. I'm also relieved that he didn't choose to put us in for 'Dog Who Most Resembles His Owner' - we might both look the image of drowned rats, but I don't need a public accolade to prove this.

And so, we sat down on bales of soggy and spiky hay to watch the professionals parade around and endure intricate inspections of goodness knows what attributes. All three of us were breathing a sigh of relief – there is no way we would have passed this test without risking becoming an impromptu comedy act.

Two hours and a whole bag of coercive treats later, it was our turn to take to the stage. First up was the class for 'Best Looking Dog'. The competition was stiff, but like a proud mother, the other dogs blended into insignificance alongside my handsome boy. Radar and I stood our ground as the judges approached and fondled each of us admiringly. When I say us, I mean the dogs. Wouldn't want to imply any suggestion of inappropriate fondling. One by one each winning candidate was called forward, but alas, Radar's beauty was not to be rewarded and we were left in the line of the merely ordinary.

Still, Radar was not to be put off. He had now got a taste for this game of being on show and so was delighted to be called up to parade once more for the all-important and final chance of glory: Dog with the Waggiest Tail.

By this point, we had got this. Hyped on treats and full of unspent exuberance, the chance to wag and express joy at every dog in the arena was Radar's chance to shine. Never had a dog wagged so hard and so long. Dragging me behind him we greeted the whole queue with loving wags and twirls and even a toothy grin or two until the competition were crushed by our wagalicious welcome.

Moments later, the results were announced.

Radar and owner Julia Day have won our final category, Dog with the Waggiest Tail!

I have *never*, and possibly will never again, experience such a moment of unadulterated pride in my dog.

Radar is a true champion of joy!

Epilogue

July 25th – 26th 2017

The dog has had the last bark and so this chapter of dog-ownership finishes on a high.

Tomorrow, Doug and I are going away on a surprise trip to celebrate our wedding anniversary. Well, I say 'surprise' - I'm pretending not to know where we are going, but I accidentally saw the itinerary pop up in our emails so am pretending that I have *no idea* that we are heading to stay on fort in the middle the Solent, now redesigned into a luxury hotel.

Radar will be cared for by Sascha and her boyfriend with a little help from Charlie and we will be home and dry within twenty-four hours.

What could possibly go wrong?

Afterword

Thank you for reading Beware of the Dog!

If you have enjoyed this book, please consider leaving a short review or star rating on Amazon to help to get this tale into the hands of many other current and future dog-parents out there.

Julia Day